Social Work Management and Practice

of related interest

Stress in Social Work
Edited by Richard L Davies
ISBN 1 85302 390 6

The Working of Social Work
Edited by Juliet Cheetham and Mansoor A.F. Kazi
ISBN 1 85302 498 8

Competence in Social Work Practice
Edited by Kieran O'Hagan
ISBN 1 85302 332 9

Learning and Teaching in Social Work
Towards Reflective Practice
Edited by Margaret Yelloly and Mary Henkel
ISBN 1 85302 237 3

Handbook of Theory for Practice Teachers in Social Work
Edited by Joyce Lishman
ISBN 1 85302 098 2

Competence in Social Work Practice
Edited by Kieran O'Hagan
ISBN 1 85302 322 9

An A–Z Community Care Law
Michael Mandelstam
ISBN 1 85302 352 3

Psychology and Social Care
Edited by David Messer and Fiona Jones
ISBN 1 85302 762 6

Community Care Practice and the Law
2nd Edition
Michael Mandelstam
ISBN 1 85302 647 6

Social Work Management and Practice

Systems Principles

Second Edition

Andy Bilson and Sue Ross

Jessica Kingsley Publishers
London and Philadelphia

First edition published in 1989 by Jessica Kingsley Publishers.

This edition published in the United Kingdom in 1999 by
Jessica Kingsley Publishers Ltd
116 Pentonville Road
London N1 9JB, England
and
325 Chestnut Street
Philadelphia, PA 19106, U S A.

www.jkp.com

Library of Congress Cataloging in Publication Data
Social work management and practice : systems principles. – 2nd ed.
1.Social service – Great Britain 2.Social work administration –
– Great Britain
I.Title II.Ross, Sue
361.3'0941

British Library Cataloguing in Publication Data
A CIP catalogue record for this book is available from the British Library

ISBN 1 85302 388 4

Printed and Bound in Great Britain by
Athenaeum Press, Gateshead, Tyne and Wear

Contents

Acknowledgements

This edition of the book has required us to reconsider many things about why we do what we do and what we believe about our work. It has been both a privilege and a struggle to complete because the lure of doing new things is so often more seductively tempting than reconsidering and reworking existing work. We have received vital encouragement from colleagues who still value the original book and who believed we should produce a second edition. Most especially we would like to thank Jessica Kingsley for her patience and flexibility in publishing schedules. We consider ourselves very fortunate in our publisher.

We want to dedicate this second edition of the book to our daughters, Emma and Anna, who, in their own remarkable ways, continue to inspire our work and our life together. The future they face will be full of complex practical, moral and ethical challenges which will require their generation to find ways of using both the feelings of their hearts and the logic of their intellects in harmony. We hope and believe that in the ideas described in this book there are signposts about the dangers society faces as well as some of the possibilities for joy and adventure for those who go where angels fear to tread.

Preface to the Second Edition

Whilst much has changed since this book was first published in 1989, we are now more convinced than ever of the need for social work to base itself on sound theoretical principles which help social workers and their managers in practice. Social work has survived many more child care inquiries since the first edition and has entered the era of community care with its new structures and forms of service delivery. Despite these changes social workers and their managers continue to be under attack and blamed for actions and inactions whether these relate to protecting children, discharging people from long-stay institutions or retaining old people at home. Within social work there was the advent of a culture of managerialism through the 1980s and early 1990s with efficiency and effectiveness chanted like a mantra for survival. At the same time, social work services exist within a harsher economic climate with a political thrust towards tougher punishment of society's 'failures', whether these are young offenders, single parents, or even elderly people who have failed to save enough money for their old age. The social work profession appears unable robustly to defend itself or to promote the positive work it does whilst workers continue to fear the worst and hope for the best in seemingly equal measure.

There are those who would say that in the face of this harshening landscape it is unrealistic to call for social work to focus on issues of theory. However, we remain powerfully committed to the importance of the need for the foundation of theory which can influence practice about change in organisations, communities and individuals without which social work is unable to assert its right to intervene in people's lives. Despite the best intentions of social workers their interventions always have the power to harm those they seek to help or protect. Only with a sound theoretical and conceptual basis for our interventions can we hope to minimise this danger. Social work managers and practitioners must have the ability to examine critically the effects of their practice. To this end we feel that the theoretical and practical proposals of this book continue to offer the best basis for consideration of issues of change in individuals, groups and organisations. At times such an analysis has to challenge orthodox views of management and practice in order to develop new directions for social work. We continue to do this not out of a desire to criticise our colleagues and our profession, but out of a concern to see social workers and those who manage social work services receive the respect and regard they deserve.

The writings of the systems theorists, particularly that of Bateson, remain particularly complex and intellectually demanding. This second edition does not add to the reader's burdens by introducing substantial new material from writers such as Humberto Maturana, though work developed by one of the writers since the first edition has concentrated substantially on the development of constructivist approaches and their implications for the application of information systems and research in the management of human services (Bilson 1995, 1996, 1997). Instead, the new edition adds references to Bateson's posthumous publications (Bateson and Bateson 1988; Bateson 1991) and refers to those who have developed ideas based on his writing in the intervening years. Chapter 3 has been substantially rewritten to describe the use of systems ideas in family therapy and the development from this to consider wider approaches to organisations. Most importantly, it briefly introduces the reader to the concept of systems as 'networks of conversations' which has done much to move systems theory beyond its original dependence on mechanistic and biological metaphors and models.

The book does not attempt to look at the writing of those who currently base their practice on postmodern ideas, as this would require the introduction of a further complex theoretical perspective and would detract from the integrity of the work as a whole. Those familiar with postmodern theories will inevitably be able to draw parallels particularly between them and Bateson's view about the nature of truth, science and reality.

Chapters 2 and 3 are amended and updated since the original edition and we make some reference to the critics of the Milan therapists who used Bateson's theoretical ideas to underpin their family therapy. In particular we were concerned that the first edition of the book did not address significantly issues of power and morality in therapeutic relationships. We have sought to address these issues in these new chapters. The issue of power was a fundamental question which Bateson and his colleagues worked on throughout his life. We believe that in understanding writers like Maturana there appear ethical and moral dimensions in considering power relationships which advance our thinking and go beyond Bateson's work. Bateson caused much confusion because of his description of power as a myth. In this he was referring to the application of a mechanistic view of power that implies the ability of one part of a system to have control over the system in which it participates, something which the reader will be encouraged to see as the antithesis of his views about the nature of systems.

There is a particular irony in the description in Chapter 7 of an organisation trying to change its policies which was itself used in evidence in the 1992 inquiry into child care policies in Fife. Readers of this book will not be surprised that ideas (or at least other people's perceptions of those ideas) are subject to scrutiny as much as are actions and events. When those ideas are seen to challenge an orthodoxy, even one so ill-defined as what constitutes the 'best interests of the child', it is perhaps inevitable that the ideas themselves can be seen as dangerous and those who attempt to describe them as zealots or professional agitators. We remain of the view that all social welfare agencies have no legitimate authority to act in the interests of others without critical debate about their processes or outcomes for those they seek to help. However difficult these debates are, particularly for those who most fear changes in practice or policy, they cannot be avoided if the social work profession is to act with integrity and purpose. History, of course, has a habit of giving a verdict on these matters. We have left the sections that deal with events in Fife largely unchanged for readers to form a judgement of our understanding of these matters written without the benefit of hindsight shortly after the events described. We have added into this chapter, however, examples of the use of systems ideas in direct management situations as well as the application at the level of organisational change. We hope these will be helpful to managers trying to deal with the range of complex tasks within social welfare agencies with all their practical, ethical and operational dilemmas and difficulties. They all come from our experience as managers in such agencies in England, Wales and Scotland.

This edition has a completely new Chapter 8 which applies systems approaches to social work education. This fundamentally challenges the current orthodoxy of competency-based training which does not equip social workers, in our view, to see their work in any holistic way and is likely to be more damaging to the ecology of clients' lives than to be of value. It proposes a model of learning based on Bateson's ideas of first-, second- and third-order learning and gives a lengthy example of the application of that theoretical model to a piece of teaching on a social work course.

It is important in this preface to outline some assumptions that underpin the whole of the approach being proposed in this book, but which it has been brought to our attention are not adequately or explicitly stated in the original. This concerns the idea of empowerment and its relationship to a systems approach. Our basic understanding of systems is based on Bateson's idea that the part cannot unilaterally control the whole. Our belief is that the organisations, families, communities and individuals with whom we work have within them the capacity for new and innovative responses to the often difficult situations with which they are faced, but they are also trapped by their own beliefs about what is possible which often excludes doing something different. The job of a social worker, manager, consultant or other person working in this situation is to find ways to help those within the system to tap into the new and different possibilities for action of which they alone are capable. This is unlikely to be achieved by simple logical explanations or by providing insight. Any approach must be based on respect for the system as a whole and the participants in it.

It is inevitable that in our reconsideration of the earlier volume we should want to revisit the final chapter and to reassess the future developments of systems ideas. This gives us the opportunity to point the reader to developments in our own practice and references to some more recent work are given. It also gives an opportunity to assess the developments which have occurred since the book was first written. Despite the time since this chapter was written, we still come back to the central dilemma for the survival of social work. This is that we are a profession which is founded on the possibility of change for individuals, groups, communities and organisations and yet without a theory, such as the one put forward in this book, we remain unable even to define the nature of change nor explain the processes through which change occurs. It is our belief that the social work profession must develop a theoretical foundation upon which it can build its credibility.

Finally, we should add that since the original edition we have received encouragement from colleagues who have used it in their work and have made comments upon it. Their impact on this second edition should not be underestimated. Through the shared search for explanations about the nature of our work in social work have come many questions about the nature of knowledge, power and human purpose that can sound very esoteric and philosophical. Yet social workers and their managers daily have to make pragmatic decisions on the basis of limited information about what will be best for their clients. We believe this book helps with those decisions, even if the journey to understand the concepts it describes can be a demanding one.

CHAPTER 1

A History of Systems Ideas in Social Work

> We might expect to find the same sort of laws at work in the structure of a crystal as in the structure of society.
>
> Bateson, *Mind and Nature (1980)*

> It is as impossible to know the parts without knowing the whole as to know the whole without specifically knowing the parts.
>
> Blaise Pascal, *Pensées Oeuvres Completes*

One of the most powerful images of British social work appeared in a cartoon in *Nalgo News.* It shows two identical scenes. In each one, the social worker is being hung on a gallows by an angry mob. The caption for the first scene reads 'Social worker who takes child from family', and for the second 'Social worker who leaves abused child with family'.

Social work, as a profession, is full of uncertainties. This is evident not just in the child abuse field but in all areas of social work. In Britain its public image seems destined to remain inexorably poor and, despite some powerful advocates within the profession, nothing seems to change this. Writing in *Community Care,* Brand wrote:

> It is arguable that social work suffers less from a bad public image than from a poor self-image. Asked at a party what they do for a living, social workers usually apologise for the job they do. They live with a chronic conflict between the profession's values and ideals and the realities of practice in under-resourced bureaucratic agencies. They work with groups whom society tends to devalue, marginalise and reject and often

> share their sense of stigma. They see the media hyping their failures, but often look in vain for positive aspects to put the case forward for social work and explain what the public can reasonably expect. (Brand 1996, p.8)

Social workers are plunged almost daily into dilemmas about when and how to intervene in other people's lives with few, if any, guiding principles on which to base an assessment of the nature of their tasks. The theory base for their actions is often drawn more from intuition or 'common sense' ideas about what should happen in certain situations than any analysis of the nature of social work.

Many writers have looked at the problems of the theory base of social work (for example Bartlett 1970; Goldstein 1973) but social workers, researchers and managers struggle when trying to define the concepts that underpin practice. Despite a large body of literature about social work practice, its theoretical underpinnings remain at best illusive, at worst non-existent. This is no abstract or trivial matter since social work repeatedly fails to cultivate underlying principles of action which govern the reasons for and the nature of delivery of services to clients. Ethical statements from the profession, such as the British Association of Social Workers' code of ethics, appear like mirages to social workers in that, when one moves towards them for guidance, the substance and foundations disappear and leave a confusing, unclear and often contradictory array of assumptions, many of which are still rooted in the practice of social casework drawn from the writers of the 1940s, 50s and 60s (such as Biestek 1957; Perleman 1957; Hollis 1972 and others). With the increased resources ploughed into social work in Britain from 1974 onwards and its very real lack of public and professional credibility, there is a pressing need to define the nature of social work and to formulate principles which underpin intervention into the lives of social work clients. To do this, fundamental questions must be asked about how individuals and societies change and develop. Without answers to these questions about the nature of our assumptions about the world, social work will repeatedly fail to define its theory or practice in any coherent or practical way and may end up truly hung by an inability to resolve the contradictions posed by whether and how to intervene in other people's lives.

The social work writers of the 1950s and 60s imply that social casework honestly, sensitively and caringly applied to people's needs will produce helpful outcomes for social work clients. Hollis's (1972) confident description of the social caseworker developing a range of techniques to help their clients demonstrates this positive philosophy based on the social worker's skill:

> Like the skier, the worker knows his general direction, but he can see only a little way ahead and must quickly adapt his technique to the terrain. To do this, he must be a skilled practitioner; he must know what to do to accomplish what and when a given procedure is necessary.

Models of social casework such as Hollis's firmly place the responsibility for effective helping on the social worker's shoulders. If the social worker has the skills, the client will be helped. These notions still powerfully affect social work training and practice at the present time. Bill Jordan (1981) says:

> I have been very conscious of the dangers of doing harm by offering incomplete or inappropriate help. I have tried to indicate that without the right combination of realism with empathy, the social worker can often, at the invitation of the client, act in a damaging and destructive way. These dangers are very much reduced if the social worker is willing to enter the client's world with him, has the courage to recognise all the horrors he sees there and the endurance to survive them. He needs both the sensitivity to perceive the whole of the client's predicament and the toughness to help him through it.

Thus, implicit in Jordan's comments is the notion that bad outcomes in social work are the result of unskilled social workers. The research into social work effectiveness suggests that, in a wide variety of fields, the confidence that social work could produce beneficial outcomes for its clients is largely unfounded. There is, for example, a large body of child care research which shows social work to be ineffective in producing any measurably successful outcomes for children and young people. Social work has been singularly ineffective in halting the passage of youngsters to custodial institutions (for example Thorpe *et al.* 1980; Giller and Morris 1981; Parker *et al.* 1981; Bilson 1986). Foster care fares little better. Research suggests that foster placements break down with alarming frequency despite the emphasis on permanency planning for children (for example Millham *et al.* 1986; Bilson and Barker 1995). Even the research on adoption shows a high breakdown rate for children placed with adoptive families. Other client groups have attracted similar research interest and it is clear that few areas of social work can confidently claim successful outcomes as demonstrated through unambiguous empirical evidence.

Such research, in addition to the almost constant bombardment of public scorn and derision for social workers in child abuse enquiries since the infamous Maria Caldwell inquiry in 1974, has resulted in a profession which appears unclear about its theoretical validity and is left only with its belief in the individual skill and responsibility of the social worker which quickly becomes blame when their interventions are seen to 'fail'.

The inquiry culture in social work produced in Scotland in October 1992 the ultimate irony of two inquiry reports being submitted to the House of Commons on the same day – one which criticised Fife social work department for failing to take enough children into care (Kierney 1992) and the Orkney Inquiry (Clyde Report 1992) into the sexual abuse of children which criticised social workers for acting too hastily in removing from home children who were believed to have been harmed or at risk. This closely mirrored the situation south of the border where inquiries such as that into the death of Jasmine Beckford, which blamed social workers for not intervening, were in sharp contrast to the Cleveland Inquiry which criticised social workers for unwarranted intervention in the lives of families.

This leaves social workers who are committed to assessing the impact of their practice feeling guilty and inadequate in the face of continuing client need. Some writers have dared to hint that there may be paradoxes inherent in social welfare which need to be understood before theoretical and practice issues can be defined. For example, Keith Wilding (1979) says of the child abuse procedures adopted by British local authorities:

> It can be argued that the system has a counter-productive effect in its attempts to help/control child abuse. It increases the pressure so much on what must be a fragile set of relationships to begin with that casework support actually contributes to such things as marital breakdown.

Similarly, research into child protection by one of the writers (Bilson and Thorpe 1998; Thorpe and Bilson 1998) has found that most child protection investigations find no abuse and end by offering apologies but little or no help even where, had no investigation been instituted, support might have been welcomed and needed (Thorpe and Bilson 1998):

> The difficulty with current child protection thinking, with its attendant theoretical assumptions about 'risk' and 'prediction,' is that it leads to expressions of concern about children being classified as 'child protection' matters. As seen in this study this leads to families being investigated rather than being offered help. However despite the

> growing evidence of the problems of this approach, challenges to it are frequently derided and attacked.

Similarly, Edgar H. Auerswald says: 'We are learning that many of the systems we have created to deliver services are, in the name of "progress" and "civilisation", contributing to the position of human distress that they were designed to alleviate' (1968). The important issue that the social worker's actions and the functions of her agency, though usually well meaning in intent, can actually create more distress and tension for a client and can serve to destroy social systems rather than restore them, has now to be part of any theoretical analysis of social work at this time, but it is rarely addressed in the literature.

This book attempts to define a theoretical basis for social work which acknowledges the social worker's power to help, as well as to destroy social systems. It will give examples which show how research can be used to guide practice rather than merely providing a negative commentary on it. It also demonstrates that at both the level of agency planning and policy and at the level of individual social work practice with clients and their families, the same theoretical underpinnings can be applied. It links the management of social work to the practice of social workers in their agencies and it is the authors' belief that the failure of social work to do this has rendered social workers powerless to withstand the variety of attacks on the profession which continue to threaten its very existence.

It is the need to determine the nature of social work intervention that prompted this book. The book does not suggest that social work can ever be free of paradoxes and dilemmas, since the power social workers and social welfare agencies have over people's lives must, of necessity, create tensions for the profession. Yet the suggested way forward of greater regulation, national standards, a General Social Services Council and privatisation of significant sections of services will not address the central question of what underpins a social worker's right to intervene in the lives of others and how should that intervention be managed at an individual and agency level. It is argued that systems ideas, which offer explanations for how change occurs, are central to the development of an approach to social work which respects and enhances the 'ecology' of the individuals, families, groups and communities with whom we work.

If an example in the natural world is considered as a metaphor for the problems of social work intervention, the following extract from the *Observer* on 1 September 1985 demonstrates the complexity of the issues.

> Deep Water Dilemma for Falmouth 'Falmouth Container Ltd ... want to see the town developed as Britain's busiest roll-on roll-off container port. This would involve filling in more than half the estuary. It would have a catastrophic effect on the environment but it does not need planning permission ... The prospect of such a massive development has split the people of Falmouth into two camps – those who believe it will create more than a thousand new jobs in an area of high unemployment – and those who fear a major ecological disaster.
>
> The latter fear severe oil pollution if the project goes ahead and possibly widespread flooding as a result of restricting the estuary. The increased tidal flow would drown some mammals and so destroy the river bed that it would take years to recover ... A naturalist ... believes the removal of large quantities of silt would have far-reaching consequences for all forms of life in the estuary. 'Just about everything in this river is dependent on everything else' he said. 'The seaweed, the crustaceans, fish and the birds are all part of a complex eco-chain which would be shattered if the project goes ahead.'

This extract describes how interventions in the natural system to try to bring new work to Falmouth would have consequences throughout the eco-system: on animal and plant life, on people who live in the area and on tourists who may choose not to visit it any more. In fact it affects all aspects of life there. The impact of any change will be felt throughout the system. The same phenomena can be identified in social work practice.

It is our premise that the way that social work problems are currently understood is fundamentally flawed. A new way of thinking is required if the ecological consequences of social work interventions are to be understood. This book will attempt to provide a framework for understanding the process of social work interventions in complex social systems. It will provide a range of systemic principles drawn from the work of Gregory Bateson and other systems writers and will look at the implications of these principles in defining the social work task with clients and within agencies. It will distil from Bateson's very wide theoretical concerns principles which are relevant to the provision of social work services and apply these to the practice of social work. The enquiry here is fundamentally about the assumptions that underpin social work practice and it is an attempt to articulate a form of practice, which we shall term 'ecological', based on these assumptions. Such an attempt will inevitably be partial, but all acts of human enquiry remain incomplete, particularly when they involve examining levels of complexity in human affairs and social situations that far exceed anything produced within a laboratory, in a test tube or in a black box. This book moves to a more precise definition of social work theory based on a systemic understanding of how social systems change and develop and how individuals within those systems are affected by and can affect those changes. Fundamental to the understanding of systems ideas is the work of Gregory Bateson.

Gregory Bateson

Gregory Bateson has been described as 'one of the most important and least understood thinkers of the 20th century' (Brockman 1977). He lived from 1904 to 4 July 1980 and was the son of the famous biologist and geneticist, William Bateson, and the husband, for many years, of Margaret Mead, the anthropologist. His contributions to anthropology, biology, psychiatry, genetics, education and ecology are considerable. His work as the leader of the research team at Palo Alto with his colleagues Jay Haley, Paul Watzlawick, Don Jackson, John Weakland and others have influenced social work through psychiatry and family therapy. His writings with Jackson and Haley about double bind theory and the way families behave are well known. Material will be drawn from three periods of Bateson and his colleagues' work. The first is his anthropological analysis of the Naven ceremony and the work of the systems scientists at the Macy conferences on feedback. The second area is the work of his research group at the Palo Alto Mental Research Institute in the 1950s and 60s and the third is his later work on ecology and social change and of those writers who contributed to the development and application of systems ideas. Included in this last period is Bateson's posthumous publication *Angels Fear* finished by his daughter Mary Catherine Bateson (Bateson and Bateson 1988). She describes this as being based on 'miscellaneous, unintegrated and incomplete' writings which were the basis for a collaboration which he intended to publish with his daughter. This book restates in very interesting literary form of the 'metalogue' many of the fundamental principles contained in *Mind and Nature* (1980).

The discovery of feedback

Bateson's first major work was *Naven* (1958), his anthropological study of the Iatmul people of New Guinea. It describes the Naven ceremony, when the young men of the village come of age. Bateson used the description of the events of the ceremony as a kind of metaphor for an analysis of the culture of the Iatmul people – how their society was structured, how it evolved and how it passed on its culture. In his preface to the 1958 edition, he added a second epilogue in which he explains the problems he left unresolved in *Naven*, which were basically how a society could split apart – what he termed 'schismogenesis' – or hold together and adapt and change to new circumstances. He described this phenomena as 'morphogenesis'. Bateson identified the Naven ceremony as the critical ritual exemplifying the possibility of fragmentation as well as the maintenance of order in their social system. In this preface Bateson (1958) refers to the part that developments in systems theory played in his thinking, saying:

> since the original publication, a new way of thinking about organisation and disorganisation had occurred and that issues in psychiatry, ecology and discussions about the organisation of society as well as anthropological data could all be approached 'through a single epistemology' – a single body of questions.

In other words, he felt that the way we understand our world has become as much the concern of science as the raw empirical data, the so-called 'facts'. The original epilogue to *Naven* makes the profound point, which Bateson continually reiterated, that the weaving together of ethos, sociology, economics and social structure described in the book is only the scientist's way of putting together a jigsaw. He felt that there cannot be, in any sense, objective data representing the 'reality' of the Iatmul people. The pieces of the jigsaw are 'cut' by the scientist as well as assembled by him/her. This idea that the social scientist creates his/her reality is fundamental to a systemic view of social work.

Bateson went on, in the years following the Second World War, to become a major contributor to a series of conferences known as the Macy conferences. The Macy group considered the implications for biology and the social sciences of what they began to term 'feedback'. Bateson's writing repeatedly stresses the importance of the issues which this group considered. In particular, how society and social systems adapted and changed and how they responded to information. The scientists involved in the Macy conferences (Norbert Wiener, Heinz Von Neumann and Warren McCulloch) aimed to produce a general science of pattern and organisation which could unify all ideas of science within general theoretical concepts. The ideas that they came up with became known as 'general systems theory', a term first used by Von Bertalanffy at the Macy conferences. Bateson believed that the achievements of the Macy group were one of the most significant events of the twentieth century.

The important paper 'What the frog's eye told the frog's brain' (Lettvin *et al.* 1959) holds keys to several of the principles of general systems theory by answering the question 'How can a frog know anything?' It suggests that all the frog's knowledge is delineated by its sensory machinery which can be investigated by experiment. The paper concluded that to understand human beings, even at a very elementary level, you have to know the limitations of their sensory input. This analysis led to their definition of meaning as being only understandable in relation to context. This was to have a profound early influence on psychiatry and still challenges conventional views held to this day in social work.

Bateson's definitions of the concepts of 'meaning', 'reality' and 'truth' are examined further in the next chapter where we will suggest that they are key principles of systemic thought which have to be understood in order to develop a coherent theoretical basis for social work practice and management.

Families and schizophrenia

After his involvement in the Macy conferences, Bateson became responsible for the research project at Palo Alto. This research group overturned a central premise of psychotherapy which was that the behaviour of the individual defined as the 'patient' was primarily related to their internal beliefs, personality and psychological make-up. Bateson's group shifted the focus to include the context of therapy – the 'rules of the game' between the therapist and the patient, and the patient and his/her family and 'natural system'. Haley (1981) described the achievements of that research group thus:

> The contribution of the project ... was the enlargement of the description to include patient and therapist and the introduction of levels into the analysis of the interchange ... With this shift, other factors in the interchange became more relevant than self-awareness as a cause of change.

The concentration in the project on the context of therapy and questions of 'identity, human purpose and existential philosophy' raised by such an examination of context meant that the results of the research challenged the theory and practice of psychotherapy and continues to challenge social work. The project did not lay down rules for therapy or concern itself with developing therapeutic methods, rather it focused on the nature of psychotherapy and communication. Some of the researchers, particularly Haley, wanted to develop these ideas into the pragmatics of therapy. Bateson opposed this because he was concerned that there would be a 'rush to the wards' to use the techniques without any attempt to understand the underlying theoretical principles. This tension between theory and practice remains a central difficulty in applying systems ideas to the practice of social work. We shall be arguing here that social workers can develop approaches based on systems ideas which are effective in helping clients to change but that they must be based on an understanding of systemic principles and cannot be ready remedies to be applied regardless of context. The danger that Bateson was concerned to avoid is a real one for social work where pragmatic actions are frequently justified as stemming from theoretical bases which have been little studied or understood. Bateson continued to raise this issue even in his last writing where he again warned against the rush to solve problems which are not sufficiently understood (Bateson and Bateson 1988):

> Behind every scientific advance there is always a matrix, a mother lode of unknowns out of which the new partial answers have been chiselled. But the hungry, over-populated, sick, ambitious and competitive world will not wait, we are told, till more is known but must rush in where angels fear to tread ... I distrust the applied scientist's claim that what they do is useful and necessary. I suspect their impatient enthusiasm for action, their raring-to-go, is not just a symptom of impatience, nor is it pure buccaneering ambition. I suspect that it covers deep epistemological panic.

Bateson's research project in Palo Alto attempted to classify communication in terms of levels – levels of meaning, levels of logical type and levels of learning. They drew on the philosophical work of Whitehead and Russell (1910). This defined the 'theory of logical types' and it challenged the reader to 'consider the set of all sets'. This riddle exposes the idea that no class of objects can also be a member of that class. Bateson remained preoccupied with the consequences of this philosophical proposition for the remainder of his life. In 1979, the year before he died, he stressed that this was no intellectual conundrum but 'the matter of their interest was vital to the life of human beings and other organisms' (1980). In the chapters that follow we will show that confusions of the type outlined by Whitehead and Russell are responsible for many of the difficulties which social workers face in applying theory to their work.

Another influential article published in 1956 by Bateson, Don Jackson, J. Haley and John Weakland was 'Toward a theory of schizophrenia'. It expressed the substance of the research group's thinking that schizophrenic behaviour arose from an inability to discriminate between levels of communication – the literal and the metaphoric. The patient had 'learnt to learn' in a context in which schizophrenic behaviours were adaptive. If the context could be explored then the mysteries of schizophrenic speech and behaviour might be understood. The Bateson group also explored how the family encouraged and even demanded on occasions that the patient show irrational behaviour. Jackson called this latter phenomenon 'family homeostasis' (Bateson *et al.* 1963). Family interaction was 'a closed information system in which variations in output or behaviour are fed back in order to correct the system's response'. The ways in which social systems such as families receive feedback about their performance are a major concern in systems thinking and we will show how important it is in social work to understand the nature of feedback. The group's article on schizophrenia has had a major influence in psychiatry and also ultimately on social work mainly because of its impact on the work of R. D. Laing, who popularised some of these theories. Bateson ironically referred to Laing as 'my chief admirer in England' and it is Laing's work with its 'anti-psychiatric' version of psychotherapy which still has influence on the teaching of social psychology in social work in Britain and elsewhere.

At the heart of the double bind theory was the notion that the messages people receive have 'meaning' only by virtue of their context. Bateson (1980) reminds us that this also is true of a 'double bind' and that it is not an actual event or thing in itself:

> To talk as though a double bind were a something and as though such somethings could be counted ... that is all nonsense. You cannot count the bats in an ink blot because there are none. And yet a man – if he be 'bat minded' – may 'see' several.

Milton Erikson's patient who sent his mother a mother's day card 'to the woman who was just like a mother to me' is a good example of a confusion (whether intentional or not) of meaning and context and such examples are not confined to families which have a schizophrenic member.

Bateson's work was most directly linked with social work during this period whilst carrying out research into communication in families. However, these ideas are of little value without the more fundamental issues of ecology described in the next section. The work of Bateson's research group at Palo Alto thus provided a different basis for understanding communication problems in families, but in order to do this it had to throw out many of the concepts established in psychiatry. The ideas developed by the research group underpin much of family therapy and the implications of systems thinking for family therapists and those working in wider systems are considered further in Chapter 3. It is possible to trace in the history of the research group at Palo Alto the tensions between the theoretical and the practical aspects of their work. These tensions are very real for all of us who work in the practical world trying to deal with the 'real' problems of everyday life.

Ecology and the application of systems ideas in social science

Bateson left the Palo Alto research group in 1963, and from that period until his death, his work moved away from ideas about communication in families, to examine the organisation of large social and natural systems – societies, cultures, the environment and the eco-system. His writings on ecology, particularly in the collection of essays entitled *Steps to an Ecology of Mind* (1973) and his book *Mind and Nature* (1980), form the two major statements of his philosophical and theoretical ideas. Their central importance to an understanding of systems ideas requires that they are described in some detail both here and in Chapter 2 which distils from them what we regard as key principles of a systems approach to social work.

Bateson's studies of the pollution of the environment led him to the belief that the world was in grave difficulties and that this required that 'the whole philosophy of government education and technology must be debated'(1973). He proposed that there were three causes of environmental difficulties which, in combination, resulted in threats to the survival of the human race. These were first, technological advances, second, population increases and third, and most importantly, 'conventional (but wrong) ideas about the nature of man and his relation to the environment'. He illustrates this by referring to the history of the insecticide DDT which was invented as an *ad hoc* measure to increase agricultural products and to save people, especially troops overseas, from malaria. He describes the invention of DDT as 'A symptomatic cure for troubles connected with the increase of population' (1973).

Bateson described how a vast industrial commitment to DDT manufacture developed. The insects at which DDT was directed became immune, whilst animals which ate the insects were contaminated. In addition, the population of the world increased because DDT reduced the number of people dying of malaria. Bateson concluded that the world became 'addicted to what was once an *ad hoc* measure' (1973); and DDT itself came to be a major danger and the effects of its use remain in the ecosystem – in the plant life, fish-eating birds, carnivorous fish and so on – for generations even after its use is discontinued. The use of DDT is one of many such *ad hoc* measures which compound rather than alleviate problems in society.

Bateson described how the increase of population spurred on the demand for technological progress and encouraged the development of the idea that human beings had 'power' over their environment which became seen as 'hostile' to their survival. He was particularly concerned to change the latter notion since he regarded it a major tenet of systemic theory that 'the creature that wins against its environment destroys itself' (1973). Bateson stressed that the way we think about our world is crucial to the way we behave towards it, since we are capable of creating havoc with the natural world and its creatures (as with the production of DDT). Bateson concludes: 'The circuits and balances of nature can too easily get out of kilter and they, invariably, get out of kilter when certain basic errors of our thought become reinforced by thousands of cultural details.'

We will suggest that similar errors of thought occur in social work and that this leads to the 'circuits and balances' of clients' systems and, at another level, of the organisational and agency systems getting out of kilter in equally disastrous ways. These matters will be examined in more detail in later chapters.

Turning to the specific literature of social work, very little use has been made of Bateson's ideas. Auerswald proposed an ecological systems approach in the field of community psychiatry in the United States. Lynn Hoffman provides a description of his approach which is similar to our own. She states (Hoffman and Long 1969) that Auerswald's approach was: 'directed at the total field of a problem, including other professionals, extended family, community figures, institutions like welfare, and all the overlapping influences and forces that a therapist working with poor families would have to contend with'.

However, the most influential exponents of systems ideas in general social work are probably Alan Pincus and Anne Minahan (1973). These writers hardly draw on Bateson and his colleagues' work for their ideas and they leave out most of the essential components of systems thinking from their analysis of social work. In particular, their work does not use concepts such as interconnectedness and feedback. In our view these issues are at the heart of ideas of change in social work and theoretical perspectives that do not address them carry a fatal flaw. Pincus and Minahan's mechanistic notions of 'target systems', 'change agents' and the like describe varied practices within welfare agencies but do not help to define the nature of social work itself. However, despite this criticism of their work, there is one article in their book which makes an important contribution to systems thinking in social work and which is particularly relevant to the ideas which we will go on to develop. This is the final article by Lynn Hoffman and Lorence Long called 'A systems dilemma', originally published in 1969 as a companion article to Auerswald's, and it merits a detailed analysis here because it raises many of the difficulties and issues presented by the application of systems concepts in social work.

Hoffman and Long's article describes 'A community health services programme designed to approach human crises as ecological phenomena; and to explore...and respond to them within this framework' (1969). They do this by the presentation of a case study: Mr Johnson, a black, poor, working-class man with a drink problem. They take their theoretical base as 'ecological systems theory' – a phrase borrowed from Gregory Bateson's work. The article attempts to address the problems of the application of systems principles. One problem is described by them as follows: 'A single person is the focus of the study, but the entire ecological field – individual within family within wider social network – is the area under consideration'.

In Mr Johnson's case, this means describing his family network, class and racial issues which create the context of his behaviour and, most importantly, the interlocking system of 'helping' agencies which combine to create and maintain his symptomatic behaviour. Hoffman and Long pose an important question: 'Does this "systems" way of looking at individual dysfunction bring with it a different way of dealing with it or is what we should be describing merely traditional social work?'.

They conclude that it is different from other forms of social work in that a new role for the social worker emerges when attempting to apply a systems approach to social work in poor communities. Perhaps the most fundamental difference between traditional social work and the activity described is that the more traditional model does not see the persons who are the helpers of a given individual or family (including the social worker) as part of the problem to be addressed: 'If reducing inequalities of power with all the interlocking systems for a distressed person is the therapeutic task, the role of the helper is going to have to be re-cast'.

Part of their 're-casting' of social work lies in their way of conceptualising Mr Johnson's problem. The actions of the welfare agencies are analysed and seen as part of the ecology which has created and maintained Mr Johnson's difficulties. Hoffman and Long draw some harsh conclusions about the welfare agency's role: 'Helping agencies have begun to carry out a coercive function beneath a genuinely charitable intent. Our national welfare system has become notorious for legislation whose overt policy seems designed to break up weak and poor families and place their members in self-perpetuating cycles of helplessness'. Hoffman and Long not only conceptualise welfare agencies as part of the problem but they also see their own work as part of the ecology of Mr Johnson's difficulties. Their dry comments about Mr Johnson's position 'hell hath no fury like a helping agent scorned' demonstrates how the attitudes and actions taken on behalf of a client can only be understood in the context of a relationship between the client and helper and how their actions are affected by the nature of this interaction. Hoffman and Long felt that: 'The communications (i.e. from helping agencies) were characterised by a confusion of benevolent/derogatory attitudes, intricately masked'.

Hoffman and Long's powerful article remains one of the few attempts to address the practice of social work within a systems framework. They strike at the heart of what we are trying to come to grips with in this book when they say, 'How to redress an imbalance of power when dealing with disturbed people and people in poor families when the presence of powerful helpers is one of the factors contributing to imbalance in the first place is the problem as it is conceived by the "systems" worker'. The contrast of their subtle attempts to unpick the complex interactions between the client and the worker and to provide systems descriptions for that work could not be more starkly drawn than in the context of the crude linear notions put forward in the rest of Pincus and Minahan's book.

The family therapy field is another major area where attempts have been made to apply Bateson's systems concepts. In this respect, the work of the Milan Associates is a major example and this is described, in detail, in Chapter 3. Family therapy remains the area within the social sciences which most clearly reflects systems ideas. There have been some developments in organisational psychology, organisational development and the management sciences to take on board some systems ideas and these are alluded to in

Chapters 4, 5 and 6 of this book. The work of organisational theorists such as Gareth Morgan and Peter Checkland, the work of Selvini-Palazzoli and Bilson applying Bateson's work to helping organisations change, are particularly relevant to our concern in this book to demonstrate how Bateson's ideas not only affect how social work should be practised, but how social work services should be organised and maintained.

Summary

Bateson's work and that of the systems thinkers challenge orthodox ways of defining and explaining the world. For this reason, Bateson's work has not had the impact it might have been expected to have upon the social sciences and on social work in particular. Bateson was described, in the 75th anniversary issue of the *Times Literary Supplement* as 'the most underrated writer of the past 75 years'. When his work is read closely, it is not difficult to understand why this might be. The wealth of scientific references are difficult for the social science reader usually unfamiliar with the physical sciences, whilst his literary allusions remain obscure to many scientific readers. The range of scientific disciplines to which he refers leaves the reader gasping and the precision and detail of his work, which is actually written in a form which attempts to define his 'new epistemology', makes rigorous intellectual demands. In *Angels Fear* he and his daughter even attempt to put forward their ideas in the 'metalogue' – a dialogue between father and daughter where each has a distinctive conversation with the other to clarify 'eternal truths' and questions. Mary Catherine Bateson admits, in her introduction to the book, that this 'groping poses a challenge to readers to make their own creative synthesis, combining his insights with the tools and information available today, advances in cognitive science, molecular biology and systems theory that are none the less still subject to the kinds of muddle and intellectual vulgarity he warned against.' (Bateson and Bateson 1988) It has to be said, however, that it is inevitable that so little of Bateson's work is known since it spans so broad a range of theoretical disciplines and is written in such complex and poetic structures and forms which leave conventional description far behind. Most of his language is complex and even his use of ordinary words like 'mind', 'love', 'wisdom' and 'the sacred' are redefined in unfamiliar ways. Bateson's work remains a profound challenge but one which we believe is important for social workers.

Bateson referred to the development of systems ideas as 'a battle'. In a letter from him to Bradford Keeney, published in 1981 after Bateson's death, he declared that 'the new thinkers' must develop 'ammunition' to confront 'the orthodoxy of scientific thought'. He speaks of the nature of the fight against orthodox scientific ideas thus (1973):

> What is interesting is that the battle is really about the choice of battlefields. Our stand is correctly and precisely upon the question: which language should be used?
>
> It was only Moloch's language that was wrong. But his choice of language vitiates (makes toxic) everything that he has been saying for 120 years. But it is a long, slow business waiting for the orthodox scientific opinion to turn – lubricating its hinges with rust solvent.

Bateson thus makes the fundamental point that any examination of the nature of social science involves questioning the basis on which that knowledge rests – its language. This need for a redefinition of the basis of knowledge is what Bateson and the systems theorists refer to repeatedly as 'epistemology'.

This book attempts to define an epistemology for social work based on concepts about how social systems change and develop. Many of the assumptions currently underlying social work practice have to be changed in such an epistemological shift. We conclude, as does Bateson, that language is the 'battlefield' upon which issues of theory and practice in social work must be fought, and we will propose the development of a new epistemology and attempt to relate it to the practice and management of social work. This approach involves changes in the way policies, resources and the planning of services should be undertaken and also requires changes in the practice and management of social work itself. Adopting a systemic epistemology is far from easy and it may be seen by some as too obscure and too speculative an exercise. Ideas in social work certainly cannot fund projects, maintain a government's commitment to social welfare, stop a parent abusing a child or provide solace to the bereaved. It is our belief, however, that social work without an ideological and theoretical foundation can never deal with the contradictions or dilemmas its practitioners and managers regularly encounter. Social work, however, has traditionally tended to prize practical ideas and techniques, but we are suggesting, as have other writers, that techniques are inadequate in the real world of human complexity. As Checkland (1972) states:

> The idea of a methodology for problem-solving in the real world is a curious one. The nature and status of such a methodology is not obvious

> ... it is not a technique. A technique is a procedure which, applied correctly in a suitable situation, will certainly produce a known result; there are techniques for making a cricket ball swing, for launching a space rocket, for handling queuing problems mathematically, and for many other activities.

Techniques, particularly written in the form of 'cook-book' descriptions of how social workers should behave in certain situations with their clients, are very popular in social work and systems ideas move against this tide of popular demand. There continue to be many methodological fads and techniques in social work which achieve popularity for a time. The use, for example, of anatomically correct dolls in working with sexually abused children (heavily criticised in the Cleveland inquiry in 1988) was one example. Similarly cognitive interviewing, social skills work, risk assessment and other techniques can also be dangerous when they do not address the contextual issues which define the client's problem. It was Keeney (1983) who said that 'We should regard any "bag of tricks" for curing and preventing pathology as ecologically dangerous, potentially leading to higher orders of problems'.

Systems ideas can provide principles on which to govern action but they cannot define models for practice in social work. What can be developed is a form of practice which considers human beings in their environment or ecology and the very nature of such an approach requires social workers to take account of the particular context of the individual. However, whilst acknowledging the difficulty of adopting a new epistemology, the acquisition of a philosophical and conceptual basis for social work of the type being proposed here is, in our view, a necessity for the survival of a credible social work profession in Britain.

CHAPTER 2

Key Principles of a Systems Approach

> Mr M'Choakumchild was explaining about National Prosperity. And he said, 'this schoolroom is a Nation. And in this nation, there are fifty millions of money. Isn't this a prosperous nation, Girl number twenty, isn't this a prosperous nation, and a'nt you in a thriving state?'
>
> 'What did you say?' asked Louisa.
>
> 'Miss Louisa, I said I didn't know. I thought I couldn't know whether it was a prosperous nation or not, and whether I was in a thriving state or not, unless I know who had got the money, and whether any of it was mine. But that had nothing to do with it. It was not in the figures at all.'
>
> Charles Dickens, *Hard Times (1854)*

In this chapter, key principles will be drawn from Bateson's work. These principles provide a foundation for a systems approach to social work and the problems it attempts to resolve. They form a basis for a different way of perceiving and thinking about the world – what Bateson termed a 'systemic epistemology'.

The premise of this book is that social work is based on a flawed epistemology. In particular there are deep errors in understandings of social systems and the way they change, and these errors lead to serious problems both in social work practice and its management. Proposing a new basis for thinking about social problems is no light undertaking. Attempting this when we continue to struggle with the complexity of adopting a systems epistemology is only justifiable because of the fruits that our own incomplete understandings have born in our work. We hope that the principles that follow and the examples of social work practice and management in later chapters will provide signposts for others who wish to undertake this journey and develop these ideas more fully. The key principles are as follows:

- circularity
- information
- epistemology
- pattern and form
- logical types
- change and stability in social systems
- power and ethics.

Circularity

The first of the key principles is that of circularity. This is a central premise from which the articulation of systems ideas flows. Bateson talks of science inheriting an Aristotelian framework of analysis in which there is an assumption that there are simple chains of causation with A leading to B and soon to C. Bateson suggests that these linear notions cannot be applied to living systems. He advocates instead a circular epistemology which acknowledges the way in which all elements of a system interact, influence and are influenced by each other. Selvini-Palazzoli and her colleagues describe this different basis for understanding interaction in relation to their therapy with families as follows (Selvini-Palazzoli *et al.* 1978):

> we must abandon the causal-mechanistic view of phenomena that has dominated the sciences until recent times, and adopt a systemic orientation. With this new orientation, the therapist should be able to see the members of the family as elements in a circuit of interaction. None of the members of the circuit have unidirectional power over the whole, although the behaviour of any one of the members of the family inevitably influences the behaviours of the others. At the same time it is epistemologically incorrect to consider the behaviour of one individual as the cause of the behaviour of the others. This is because every member influences the others, but is in turn influenced by them.

In general in human and biological systems we deal with sequences that resemble stimulus-and-response rather than cause-and-effect. When one billiard ball strikes another there is a transfer of energy such that the motion of the second ball is energised by the impact of the first ball. In social systems this is not the case. If a man kicks a dog, the dog's behaviour, unlike the billiard ball, is not directly determined by the force of the kick. If the dog chooses to turn and bite the man it is likely that an observer would say that the man had caused the dog to bite him because of his kick. On the other hand if the dog chooses to run away the man's kick could equally well be described as the cause. In the dog-plus-man system the outcome is dependent on a set of issues extending far beyond the stimulus. These include the learned behaviours of the dog and the man; the history of their interaction; contextual factors and numerous other interacting elements of the man-plus-dog system which form the context of their current interaction.

An example of the contrast between a linear analysis and a circular one can be seen in a patient's problem behaviour in psychiatry. In a linear analysis, a patient's problem behaviour might be seen as a result of a 'cause' in the past, perhaps during his childhood, when some trauma, or event, or feeling, had to be relegated to his unconscious mind. Its repression thus leads to symptomatic distress. In traditional psychotherapy the etiology of the illness or problem would be sought through a series of attempts to describe how it feels and its treatment would involve various methods including analysis, history taking, discussion and medical tests – depending on the training and the professional and personal beliefs of the psychiatrist.

An application of circular thinking would concern itself with developing a hypothesis about the way that behaviour is maintained within the system of which the patient is a part (usually the family and wider social system) and the functional nature of the symptom for each member of that system. The question would not therefore be 'why does it occur?', but 'how does the behaviour affect all parts of the system and what system's dilemma is solved by its existence and continuation?' In the case of, for example, a child's developing night terrors which involved the parents in a repeated pattern of allowing the child to sleep with them, a circular analysis would not focus on the original 'cause' of the behaviour. Rather it would focus on what interactions in the family maintain the behaviour. It might be that the child's presence enables the couple to avoid intimacy. The context of the behaviour would be the key to explaining and ultimately changing it. There would be no need to search for root causes in the past. Its relational significance on the behaviour, attitudes and opinions of others would be central. The behaviour of the afflicted person would be seen as part of a wider 'dance' (to use Minuchin's (1974) word) which is locked into the repertoire of the family system.

Most modern psychiatric thinking, and therefore much of social work, has inherited an Aristotelian framework for viewing problem formation. Parents are seen as having fixed characteristics (i.e. personalities) which act on their children and cause certain outcomes. Laing's notion of schizophrenogenic families is a clear example with its implications that parents drive their offspring mad. In social work, the same linear epistemology applies and a cursory glance at any case file will yield examples such as the following:

> With the family history of violence and alcoholism it is hardly surprising the boy offended.
>
> The children came from a deprived home in a run-down and alienated community which contains a large number of multi-problem families where offending is common.
>
> He started offending when his father left home because of his role-confusion at that time.
>
> He acted out his unresolved grief about his grandfather's death by missing school.
>
> After her miscarriage Mrs S could not cope with the pressures on her in the family.

Statements of this kind imply that there is a direct causal link between an individual's behaviour and, for example, the norms of the local community. Such explanations imply an element of determinism which is only possible with the aid of hindsight. Bateson claimed that 'linear thinking will always generate either the teleological fallacy (that end determines process) or the myth of some controlling agency' (1980) and clearly he saw it as a major flaw in our understanding of science and the organisation of matter. The difficulty that Bateson himself acknowledges is in describing circular ideas in a language which itself has a linear structure. This severely limits the ability to move out of a linear frame of reference. As he says in *Mind and Nature* 'language commonly stresses only one side of any interaction' (1980). In the example of the child with night terrors, the behaviour could be seen as the 'cause' of the parents lack of intimacy or vice versa, yet in systems terms neither description is 'true' – they are merely punctuations of sequences of events affecting and being affected by all aspects of the social system.

The family therapists at the Family Institute in Milan refer in their work to the problem of trying to describe circular concepts in a language which is essentially linear in character. Selvini-Palazzoli *et al.* (1978) talk of a 'linear conditioning' which human beings possess, which encompasses ideas in a linear static epistemology rather than a 'systemic circular sense which can portray the interacting nature of feedback on behaviour' . They say, 'We are imprisoned by the incompatibility between two primary systems in which human beings live: The living system dynamic and circular and the symbolic system (language) descriptive, static and linear' .

This is one of the essential problems which face those wishing to undertake a systems approach. The psychiatrist Taylor said 'Even trying to write down this complex array of interlocking cycles makes me impatient with the limitations of our language' (1979) Not only is language linear in its nature but as Dell (1982) and others have pointed out, Western thinking is primarily dominated by an Aristotelian-Cartesian-Newtonian epistemology which assumes linear notions of the world: what is real can be measured and assessed on a variety of quantitative dimensions. In this view predictability of outcome is possible. For example, a ball in a six-cushioned billiard shot can be returned to its original position by applying to it the same quantity of force and spin in the opposite direction. This linear empiricism is contrasted by what Dell describes as the 'epistemology of pattern' found in Western thinking of Pythagoras, Plato and Gnosticism, which concerns itself with what Bateson calls the 'pattern that connects'.

The principle of circularity suggests that an understanding of the interactions and behaviour of members of social systems needs to be based on the acknowledgement of their interconnectedness and that this cannot be explained in terms of linear notions such as cause and effect. We will go on to demonstrate in later chapters how the understanding of circularity in social systems affects both the practice of social work and the way services need to be structured, organised, monitored and managed.

Information

When elements of a system interact they exchange information. In this sense information is the currency of interaction. However, it is important to consider the nature of information. Bateson suggests that information is produced by the creation of 'news of difference'. Differences only occur when at least two things are compared and it is the observer making the comparison who decides what is 'news'.

In describing 'difference' Bateson is not referring to a concrete, material thing placed in time or space (1980):

> A difference is not material and cannot be localised. If this apple is different from that egg, the difference does not lie in the apple or in the egg, or in the space between them ... Difference cannot be placed in time. The egg can be sent to Alaska or can be destroyed and still the difference remains. Or is it only the news of difference that remains? Or is the difference ever anything but news? With a million differences between the egg and the apple, only those that become information make a difference.

The idea that it is difference that is the basis for information marks a major difference between the physical and the natural sciences. As Keeney (1983) says: 'in the world of pattern, events are primarily triggered by difference rather than force and energy. The invitation you didn't receive (as well as the invitation you thought you would receive) is a difference that can trigger your interaction with a party's host.' However, what is exchanged in interaction is not the difference itself but rather 'news' of the difference. When your hand is plunged into a bucket of ice it is the news of the change in temperature that is conveyed by the nervous system to the brain, not the change in temperature itself.

However, as the extract from Bateson quoted earlier shows, there are literally millions of differences capable of being perceived in any situation and the vast majority of these remain unseen – these are the differences that do not make a difference and therefore are not information. This concept of 'news of difference that makes a difference' is central to Bateson's thought. It is also supported by research into neurophysiology and perception. A common experience is the notice we take when a fan heater has been turned off. We hear the difference between the noise and the absence of noise. Another example is that if we look at the same image on a page for a long time, aspects of it, or all of it if it is really stable, become invisible and only when we look away and return to it can we see it again. To keep the perceptual world visible our eyes continually change their position. We create a system whereby different images are made in order to perceive a stable world. Keeney (1983) sums this up by saying: 'In general, every perception we are aware of is constructed from multiple views of the world. In order to see any pattern, different models of the pattern must be drawn.'

A corollary of the principle of 'news of difference' is that all information is relational and that it relates specifically to the context in which it occurs. Unlike the physical sciences where a force of zero causes no acceleration, even the absence of behaviour can create information. In addition it is the recipient who chooses to respond to the news of difference and thus ascribes meaning to it (Bateson 1980):

> The letter that you do not write, the apology you do not offer, the food that you do not put out for the cat – all of these can be sufficient and effective messages because zero, in context, can be meaningful, and it is the recipient of the message who creates the context. This power to create context is the recipient's skill.

This idea that meaning is the creation of the recipient of information is a central one to a systems approach and an important one in social work. It challenges notions such as assessment and diagnosis since in social systems the meanings being attributed are the creation of the observer. Similarly, the notion of an objective research base is challenged. We shall show how the introduction of information into family systems and larger social systems such as the 'care system' for children can bring about substantial change if it constitutes 'news of difference'.

Embedded in the concept of 'news of difference' is that of double description. Bateson (1980) asked: 'What bonus or increment of knowing follows from combining information from two sources?' He answers his own question by saying that it is not simply that two descriptions are better than one but that 'the combination of diverse pieces of information define *an approach of very great power*'. He goes on to suggest that double description is not only the basis of how organisms perceive the world around them or themselves as part of that world, but also that it provides clues and pointers to ways we can understand our world.

The fundamental premise of double description is that the difference between the two descriptions creates information about what is being described which is of a new order or dimension. Bateson illustrates this rather complicated notion through a series of examples and metaphors. He suggests that vision in animals is greatly improved by the presence of two eyes and yet points out that the information gained from either eye is fairly similar. However, from the combination of these two viewpoints the animal is able to perceive depth – a new dimension of vision created from the difference between the two images.

Descriptions drawn from different senses can also create new information. For example, if you are sitting on a train in a station and looking at another train standing alongside, when one of the trains starts to move it is often difficult for a brief period to determine whether it is your train or the other one which is moving. However the feeling of motion or its absence soon gives the necessary extra description which allows you to perceive the 'reality' of the situation.

Double description is crucial in social work, since it is the basis of the identification of the relationship between parts of a system. As Keeney (1983) says: 'Double description is an epistemological tool that enables one to generate and discern different orders of pattern ... As two eyes can derive depth two descriptions can derive pattern and relationship.'

In family therapy consultants behind a one-way screen provide a description of the events that occur on the other side of the screen which, when combined with the description of the therapist working with the family, provides new information about the family-plus-therapist system. R. D. Laing found that the description of families of schizophrenics which was gained from verbal communication was enhanced when this was put alongside a description of their non-verbal or analogic communication. For example, a father might tell a social worker that he and his wife agree on how to discipline their children but he might, through non-verbal messages, encourage his children to disobey, contradict and make fun of his wife in front of the social worker. From this combination of verbal and non-verbal communication information is gained about the relationship pattern which in this example could be described as a double bind (the juxtaposition of conflicting messages).

Double description, which requires comparisons of at least two descriptions of the system, is needed both in direct work with clients and for the better management of services. Later chapters will describe how the concepts of double description and information can be used in social work settings.

Epistemology

Bateson defines epistemology more broadly than in its usual philosophical usage. He uses it to cover two concepts; the first relates to questions such as how things are, what is a person and what sort of world is this (what philosophers would refer to as problems of 'ontology') and the second is the more usual use of epistemology as relating to questions about how we know anything or, more specifically, how we know what sort of world it is and what sort of creatures we are. Bateson (1980) states:

> There seems to be no convenient word to cover the contribution of these two concepts. The nearest approximations are 'cognitive structure' or 'character structure', but these terms fail to suggest that what is important

> is a body of habitual assumptions or premises implicit in the relationship between man and environment, and that these premises may be true or false. I shall therefore use the single term 'epistemology' ... to cover both aspects of the net of premises which govern adaptation (or maladaptation) to the human and physical environment.

A key aspect of our epistemology concerns issues of objectivity. According to Bateson it is vitally important to be aware that there is no objective experience. He stresses that this is true of all our experience even at the apparently real level of immediate sensations (1980): 'When someone steps on my toe, what I experience is not his stepping on my toe, but my image of his stepping on my toe reconstructed from neural reports reaching my brain somewhat after his foot has landed on mine.'

Bateson began his talk to the Second Conference on Mental Health in Asia and the Pacific by asking his audience whether they agreed with the proposition that 'you see me'. When many of the audience raised their hands indicating their agreement he pointed out that in fact they did not 'really' see him. What they 'saw' was a bunch of pieces of information about him that they synthesised into an image of him and that each of them created his or her own image. This apparently simple proposition that 'I see you' is in fact based on a flawed epistemology. Bateson suggested that these flaws had major consequences for societies and the future of the ecosystem despite the fact that in most day-to-day circumstances they appear to work. As he said to the delegates at the conference (1973):

> You and I are able to get along in the world and fly to Hawaii and read papers on psychiatry and find our places around these tables and in general function reasonably like human beings in spite of very deep error.

Bateson illustrates the lack of objective experience by drawing an analogy with the work of Adalbert Ames on vision and perception. Ames set up a series of experiments in an empty apartment in New York City which distorted what the subject in the experiment 'saw'. Ames's experiments were rather like a series of experiences such as the example of the two trains in a station. They were set up to distort perception of distance and depth by creating experimental situations which altered the rules which the brain uses to assess distance – the size of the image, parallax, brightness – and they thus distorted the observer's view of the world. In all the experiments the observer was first of all shown the 'real' situation before undertaking the experiment but, once participating, still saw the optical illusions. For example, in one experiment a box of matches and a box of cigarettes were made to appear to be in different positions and to be of different sizes by moving them sideways as the observer's eye moved sideways and thus changing their apparent parallax (distant objects appear to move with the observer whilst nearer objects are left behind). Despite having observed the size of the objects and their distance from the observer prior to the experiment the subject is still unable to 'see' them as they are once participating – the image of one being magnified and the other reduced. Thus even the knowledge that what is observed is not accurate or true does not enable the observer to see through the illusion.

These experiments had a profound impact on Bateson. The Ames experiments suggested to Bateson that the 'truth' about his experience of the world was an artistic creation of his own and thus notions of 'objectivity' became redundant (1980):

> The word 'objective' becomes, of course, quite quietly obsolete; and at the same time the word 'subjective', which normally confines 'you' within your skin, disappears as well. It is, I think, the debunking of the objective that is the important change. The world is no longer 'out there' in quite the same way that it used to seem to be.

This concept of the impossibility of 'objective' experience is particularly important when thinking about the nature of research and indeed of all observations in social work. Whilst at an intellectual level the lack of objectivity would be acknowledged by most people working in social work, much of social work practice is carried out as if objectivity, if not possible, is at least approachable and desirable. Social work assessments are not simple observations since they usually offer interpretations of behaviour which occurs in particular contexts. When social work is carried out on the basis of false assumptions about the 'reality' of experience it becomes impossible to extract descriptions from their context. For example, social workers often refer to 'unmotivated' clients as if such a description revealed a truth about the client rather than it being a way of describing the social worker's perception of the client's response to him/her. When it is suggested that such interpretations are not 'truths', a common response is to suggest that other interpretations would not be 'authentic' or 'honest'. Yet it is common, in our experience, for one social worker's unmotivated client to be cooperative with another worker.

Bateson suggests that because of their failure to acknowledge these epistemological problems the behavioural sciences have created loosely defined explanatory notions such as 'ego', 'anxiety', 'constraint', 'purpose', 'mind', 'motivation' and so on. He strongly attacks them, calling them a 'jungle of half-baked hypotheses' and saying that, 'in truth, most of them are so loosely derived and so mutually irrelevant that they mix together to make a sort of conceptual fog which does much to delay the progress of science' (1975) Watzlawick, one of Bateson's colleagues at Palo Alto, suggests that the implications of accepting our part in the creation of experience would be that (Watzlawick, Weakland and Fisch 1974):

> Such a person would be tolerant ... If we know that we do not or cannot know the truth, that our view of the world is only more or less fitting, we will find it difficult to ascribe madness or badness to the world views of others ...

Thus this principle, according to Watzlawick, leads to a statement close to one of social work's ethical principles – to be non-judgemental. However, it also brings into question the basis of much of the theory and practice of social work.

In a systems framework it is important to recognise the 'relativity' of observations and that they are not ultimate truths. Later chapters will show that understanding the lack of objective experience can help social workers to respond to clients or within organisations in ways which can 'unstick' problems and promote adaptation and change. Bateson talks about culture in organisations, families and teams as being 'local epistemologies' – sets of assumptions which shape how we perceive our world and the actions it is possible for us to take. Thus Bateson says of the concept of culture applied to families, communities and groups: 'One meaning of that overworked word is the local epistemology, the aggregate of presuppositions that underlie all communication and interaction between persons' (Bateson and Bateson 1988).

Thus epistemological issues apply not only to basic understandings of 'truth' and 'objectivity', but also apply to our day-to-day dealings in social work. The 'presuppositions' or assumptions we hold as teams or work groups, like those about distance in the Ames' experiments, are frequently invisible and unchallenged or 'left unexamined in the immediacy of action' (Bateson and Bateson 1988). Despite this they shape our perception and frame the possible actions we are able to take.

Pattern and form

Bateson draws another distinction between the world of living things, organisations, interactional systems and that of the 'pleroma' – his term borrowed from Jung for the world of objects and physics. He suggests that in the living world the key issues are of pattern and form rather than quantity and logic. This is of fundamental importance in understanding interactional systems and the failure to take into account the implications of this is a major flaw in many of the theoretical approaches of the social sciences. Bateson (1980) states: 'the search to split up, quantify the universe, to understand it through its component parts cannot describe or cope with the need for interconnectedness in existence.'

There are many examples within social work and the social sciences of attempts to analyse situations of complex human interaction by trying to split it down into its component parts or individual variables. For example, over the last 30 years a considerable body of literature and research in the social groupwork field has developed, analysing leadership behaviour in groups which demonstrates this point well. Leadership has been analysed and measured or described in terms of its supposed component functions and behaviours (Bales, Hare and Borgatta 1955). In this analysis leadership behaviour is seen as a distribution of functions within a group, not as part of a system of interacting behaviours which affect and are affected by all members of the group as well as the context of the group. This has meant that leadership acts in groups have come to be seen as stereotyped and limited to a series of functions and this has, through the concentration on function alone, contributed to a sterility of theory and practice in the field of social groupwork and its understanding of the nature of leadership within groups. As Keeney (1983) says: 'Leadership, in other words, is an extracted half of the double description "leader-follower relationship". In general all descriptions of personality characteristics consist of extracted halves of larger relationship patterns.' Thus 'leadership' cannot be understood without an examination of the context in which some people lead and others follow. The complementarity of these behaviours is the basis for understanding 'leadership' in its particular context.

Bateson goes further to suggest that patterns are not simply a way of understanding systems but are the very basis of identifying something as a system. Interconnectedness is at the heart of systems theory and Bateson suggests that it is 'pattern that connects'. In fact, 'The Pattern Which Connects' was an alternative title for his book *Mind and Nature*, and this indicates the central importance which he ascribes to pattern. It is the relationship between the parts of anything that gives it meaning as a system and the organisation of these parts of the system is the 'pattern which connects'.

The need to identify pattern and form rather than quantity will be addressed in relation both to understanding complex human systems and to bringing about change within those systems, particularly in attempting to introduce services for particular groups of social work clients. It is Bateson's concern that patterns should be identified, rather than that the component parts of the world should be separated, that constitutes the essential difference between a systems perspective and that of other views of social change. Thus we are advocating an approach to social work based not on splitting up and analysing social work practice and management out of the context in which it exists, but rather on an 'ecology' of social work which takes into account issues of pattern and form.

Logical types

Russell and Whitehead's theory of logical types (Whitehead and Russell 1910) had a profound influence on the thinking of Bateson and his colleagues at the Palo Alto Mental Research Institute. Bateson has used it as a metaphor to guide his thinking when confronted with apparent paradoxes which stem from self-reference in communication and later as a model for his consideration of issues of form and process in thought.

For example, it is easy to see the paradoxical nature of the statement written on a chalkboard which states that 'any statement written on this chalkboard is untrue'. If the statement is true then it is untrue and if it is untrue then it is true. The paradox is generated because this statement mixes logical types because it is both a statement and a statement about statements and it thus qualifies itself. A similar paradox occurs when a father tells his truant son not simply to go to school but that he should want to do so. If the boy attends school because he has been told to he has still disobeyed because he did not want to. The Palo Alto group call this a 'be spontaneous' paradox, because the fact that the father has requested that the boy should change means that this cannot be done spontaneously.

Bateson felt that the theory of logical types was 'vital to the life of human beings and other organisms' (1980). The theory of logical types stemmed from problems of self-reference in set theory and provided Bateson with a way of thinking about self-reference in the biological world. In particular,

Bateson was interested in self-reference in language and communication. For example, he repeatedly considers the fact that 'the name is not the thing named, and the name of the name is not the name' (1977). He felt that errors of logical typing (what might be termed category errors) were an important issue in his epistemology. He developed a model of learning based on hierarchies which is discussed more fully in Chapter 8, as well as the double bind model of schizophrenia[1] which was based on the idea of conflicts between different levels of communication.

There is no such thing as a simple statement in human communication; every message is qualified by a message on a different level. For example, if a mother says to her child 'Stop shouting', the manner in which she says it and the context within which it is said will qualify for the child the likely consequences of non-compliance.

Bateson related the theory of logical types to Alfred Korzybski's statement that 'the map is not the territory and the name is not the thing named'. He likens the confusion between different orders of 'logical type' to the error of assuming that the name of something is the thing itself, 'eating the menu card instead of the dinner' or assuming that saying 'let's play chess' is a move in the game of chess. He proposed that the confusion of logical types in human communication leads to paradoxes and that these paradoxes are far from rare in human affairs.

Bateson identified common patterns of communication between schizophrenic patients and their family as a 'double bind' which confused logical types, and in his later work he blamed errors of typology for major mistakes in areas of science, religion, philosophy and art.

1 In *Double Bind*, 1969 (Bateson 1973) Bateson describes the double bind theory of schizophrenia saying that 'Double bind theory asserts that there is an experimential component in the determination or aetiology of schizophrenic symptoms and related behaviour patterns.' The double bind that he refers to is a communicational pattern in which the schizophrenic is repeatedly faced with communications in which an overt message (e.g. verbal communication) is given in a context (e.g. non-verbal communication) which contradicts it. The two messages, which are seen as being of different logical types, place the schizophrenic in a no-win situation and he or she learns to respond with metaphorical communications which escape the dichotomy. In proposing this model Bateson was not suggesting that there was no genetic element to schizophrenia nor that anyone continually experiencing double binds would necessarily become schizophrenic, in fact, he suggests that such logical confusions can also lead to creativity such as that found in poets and comics.

Watzlawick *et al.* (1974) applied the theory of logical types to their thinking about change in human systems. They suggest that there are two types of change, one where the arrangement of the system remains unchanged and one where the system itself is changed. Watzlawick *et al.* call these respectively the concepts of first- and second-order change. They give an example of a man having a nightmare. In his dream he can run away, jump off a cliff, scream, hide, fight etc., but none of these behaviours will lead to a termination of the nightmare. This is first-order change. To achieve a second-order change he must wake up. Waking is a different state and involves a 'change of change'. The second-order change is always in the nature of a discontinuity or a logical jump and its manifestations often appear illogical or paradoxical.

Watzlawick *et al.* relate the story about the commandant at the castle of Hochosterwitz which was besieged and was rapidly running out of food. Rather than continue to ration the dwindling supplies, he solved the problem by instructing his men to feed all the remaining corn to their last pig and to propel the well-fed pig over the castle walls to the surrounding army. When this seemingly paradoxical act was done the enemy assumed that if they had food to throw away then the siege was in vain so they went home. This clearly differentiates between a first-order solution to his problem which would have been to continue to ration his people as long as possible and a second-order solution which attempted a redefinition of the nature of the struggle.

They are thus suggesting that systems can run through an infinite number of internal changes and achieve only more of the same without ever arriving at a resolution of the impasse. This first-order ability of systems to change without a change can be seen in all kinds of human activities. It is particularly clear when a family's inability to cope with stress is responded to by a supportive intervention from social workers to which the family responds by increased dependency in a 'more of the same' loop to which social workers respond by increasing contact and so on.

Likewise, there is the well-recognised phenomenon in organisations whereby seemingly constant restructuring and reorganisation are taking place but where the people working for that organisation remain as discontented, confused, uninvolved, dissatisfied and unaffected by the process of change as they always were. This is humorously referred to in management literature as the 'rearranging-the-deckchairs-on-the-Titanic' phenomenon. The 'metarules' for systems change or second order change are that change occurs when the system has to adapt and when the rules governing the system are changed.

Problems caused by confusing logical types such as maps and territories or objects and their names are common in social systems and many attempts to bring about change fail, either because they are 'more of the same' or because they request not simply that change takes place but that it does so spontaneously. This is a crucial issue in understanding the contribution of systems theory to social work, as will be shown in the chapters that follow.

Break-up, stability and change in social systems

Stability and change are important issues in social work. A variety of theories of change form a major part of social work training. The very basis of social work is the need to enable change whether it is at an individual, community or societal level. Watzlawick *et al.* sum up the paradoxical nature of the search for theories of change (1974):

> With change such a pervasive element of existence, one might expect that the nature of change and of the ways of effecting it should be clearly understood. But the most immediately given is often the most difficult to grasp, and this difficulty is known to promote the formulation of mythologies. Of course, our theory of change is yet another mythology; but it seems to us that, to paraphrase Orwell, some mythologies are less mythological than others. That is, they work better than others in their specific life contexts.

Watzlawick *et al.* go on to outline the need to consider change in relation to stability. In considering stability Bateson once again draws a distinction between the world of physics and of nature (1980):

> But the rock's way of staying in the game is different from the way of living things. The rock, we may say, resists change; it stays put, unchanging. The living thing escapes change either by correcting change or changing itself to meet the change or by incorporating continual change within its own being. 'Stability' may be achieved either by rigidity or by continual repetition of smaller changes, which cycle will return to a status quo ante after every disturbance. Nature avoids (temporarily) what looks like irreversible change by accepting ephemeral change.

A family is a clear example of a social system that has to change and adapt in order to maintain stability. The membership of families changes over time;

children are born, people join through marriage, whilst other members leave or die. As well as changes in membership families have to adapt to changes in their environment, the society or community of which they are a part. Throughout this adaptation and change families maintain some stability of beliefs, shared values, culture and so on.

The duality of stability and change is captured in a statement by Bateson (1973): 'all change can be understood as the effort to maintain some constancy and all constancy is maintained through change.' A metaphor for stability in systems which is often quoted by the systems writers is the acrobat on the high wire. She corrects her balance by constant careful movements of her body, her pole, her feet on the wire, and yet manages to move along the wire. The other side to this ability to maintain stability through constant imbalance is that systems also change, and adapt to changes in their environment through a similar process of adjustments corrected by feedback.

However, systems also break up and fragment and form new adaptations through the process of 'runaway' or 'schismogenesis'. Bateson described in *Naven* (1958) the way that the Iatmul youths were continually boasting and, if their fights became uncontrolled, broke away from the main village into the jungle, taking their family to set up a new tribal village. This process was ritualised so that the fights were an accepted part of community life and aided survival and development. He says 'Every human organisation both shows the self-corrective characteristic and has the potential for runaway' (1973).

The linking of change and stability is at the heart of systems thinking and has been alluded to by a number of writers. For example, Keeney and Ross point out the connection between this idea and that of double description (1985):

> From the point of view of double-description, change and stability are seen as two sides of a cybernetic complementarity: families cannot be described as changing without consideration for their stability and vice versa. Thus the French proverb; the more things change, the more they remain the same, can be stood on its head: the more things remain the same, the more they are changing. The tightrope walker must continuously sway to remain in balance; the way to remain balanced while standing in a canoe is to make it rock. Applying this perspective to social systems, Bateson proposes, 'You can't have a marriage and not quarrel with your wife'.

This complementarity between stability and change has also been alluded to by Watzlawick *et al.* as 'the paradoxical relationships between persistence and change' (1974), and the duality of change and stability is a crucial issue in family therapy where families presenting themselves for therapy are conceived of as asking to change whilst remaining the same. Keeney and Ross describe it thus (1985): 'In therapy, the troubled system can be depicted as communicating a message that requests stability of the system's survival or identity whilst communicating another message that requests change in the particular way it maintains itself.'

This phenomenon is a familiar one to social workers who are asked for help by clients but then discover that the client wishes, just as strongly, to remain unchanged by social work intervention. Likewise, social work agencies often accept research into their services but rarely accept changes as a result of it.

Some writers, particularly in the family therapy literature, call the tendency of systems to seek stability and order 'homeostasis'. This term enjoyed considerable favour during the 1970s, but was powerfully attacked by a number of writers including Paul Dell (1982) who calls it: 'an epistemologically flawed concept that has repetitively been used in the service of dualistic, animistic and vitalistic interpretation of systems. Accordingly, homeostasis has led to quirky clinical formulations and a great deal of fuzzy theorising.'

Bateson, with his research group colleagues Jackson, Haley and Weakland in 1956 described the family as 'an error-activated, self-correcting, homeostatic system' (Bateson *et al.* 1956), and much of family therapy theory and practice following that article developed models based on mechanistic notions of family homeostasis, which described homeostasis as a kind of thermostat switching into action to keep the temperature of a family constant when family members were trying to change their behaviour. Paul Dell suggests that this notion of family homeostasis as a kind of governor of a steam engine or the thermostat in a heating system has hampered the development of a systems epistemology based on coherence – the notion that stability and change are inextricably linked. Bateson's later work, particularly *Mind and Nature*, stresses the importance of seeing change and constancy as part of the same process and he draws an analogy with the natural world (1980):

> Survival depends upon two contrasting phenomena or processes, two ways of achieving adaptive action. Evolution must always, Janus-like,

> face in two directions: inward toward the developmental regularities and physiology of the living creature and outward towards the vagaries and demands of the environment.

Thus social systems are never actually static but are in a continuous process of change, some of which maintains stability, some adaptation. This view of change, stability and break up of systems is fundamental to the task of those wishing to assist social systems, whether they be families or social work organisations, to adapt and change.

Power and ethics

The concept of power has been at the centre of debate in the field of social work, as in other fields. Discussing this concept is not simple. For example, whilst there is an increasing focus on the concept of power in the field of organisation studies, there is no agreed definition of it (Morgan 1986). Morgan (1993) points to the way that analysis in terms of power can lead to feelings of futility and disempower those wanting to attempt change:

> Like those writers who emphasise how the social construction of reality is embedded in deeper power relations, I too believe that we act on a stage shaped by deeply ingrained assumptions and discourses, where certain groups and individuals have much greater power than others to shape the infrastructure of what we do. Knowledge of these deeper power relations can be instructive. But the image that we live in a world shaped by forces over which we have little control is generally overwhelming. It tends to create complacency and feelings of futility.

This section considers the implications of the issue of power for a systems approach and suggests that ethics provide a better basis for dealing with oppression than analysis based on power. In order to do this it is first necessary to review Bateson's view of power as a 'false' epistemology.

The controversy that has continued with regard to the concept of power is a major issue for the application of a systems approach. A major rift between Bateson and Jay Haley, with whom he developed the double bind theory of schizophrenia, stemmed from a fundamental difference over the place that issues of power have in therapy. The issue was a serious one for Bateson and, commenting on Haley's account of the double bind research group, Bateson says (1981):

> Haley slides too lightly over very real epistemological differences between himself and me. As I saw it, he believed in the metaphor of

> 'power' in human relations. I believed then – and today believe even more strongly – that the myth of power always corrupts because it proposes always a false (though conventional) epistemology.

Haley used power as a central theme of his understanding of the motivation that led to the organisation of family systems. He saw power as an attribute of organisation and stated that human beings 'cannot not organise' ... 'and that organisation is hierarchical' (Haley 1976a). Similarly he stated that human beings 'form a status, or power, ladder in which each creature has a place in the hierarchy' (1996b).

On the other hand, Bateson viewed the use of the concept of power in the natural world as an epistemological error, and an important error which led to ways of thinking and acting, that threaten the survival of humanity. Bateson writes of the application of the term power to human relationships (1973): 'probably most people believe in it. It is a myth which, if everybody believes in it, becomes self-validating. But it is still epistemological lunacy and leads inevitably to various sorts of disasters.' This disagreement about power came to light during the research into schizophrenia in the 1950s and has been an issue in family therapy since, often leading to vitriolic exchanges such as that between Dell (1986a) and Imber-Black (1986a). The centrality of this debate can be seen from the number of contributions which comment on the subject (for an overview see Bilson 1996).

Bateson's rejection of the metaphor of power in human relations concerns the way in which relationships are viewed. A view of relationships based on power is referred to as lineal causality, a term used to suggest that to view one party to a relationship as having power over another is an incomplete description which assumes a linear notion of cause and effect. This criticism of the use of the metaphor of power in human relationships has resonance with Foucault's criticism of the dominant conceptual model for power. Foucault suggests that this view of power uses the analogy of a physical force which can be applied to bodies to make them change direction, make them move or accelerate. It is this linear view of power that both Bateson and Foucault reject (Dávilla 1993).

In Bateson's view causal chains in the natural world are always circular or more complex. For example, in order for a violent husband to control his wife he has to respond to her reactions to his attempts to control. If she tries to leave he has to stop her or to follow her and force her to return to him, and she in turn responds to his responses. The particular pattern of interaction which occurs is thus not unilaterally determined by the husband. In this sense the pattern can be described as being one of circular or mutual causality. That is, the husband alone cannot determine the future pattern of their interactions; this time it might be just too much, and she may shoot him, go to a refuge, cut off his penis with scissors, or make a complaint to the police, etc.

This view of mutual or circular causation has sometimes been interpreted to mean that the parties are equally to blame for their violent interactions. However, this confuses the observation of a pattern of interactions with the making of a moral judgement. Furthermore, Bateson is not condoning this violence by observing that it consists of an interlinked pattern of behaviours. In fact it is patterns of this sort that he would see as being the result of the man's belief that he can control his wife and are thus a result of the false epistemology of power.

The interpretation of circular causation meaning that family therapists should ignore oppressive behaviour led Goldner (1985) to raise the question:

> how are we to explain the complacent brand of moral relativism that allows family therapists, even now, to pervert the concept of circularity by confusing an elegant truth, that master and slave are psychologically interdependent, with the morally repugnant and absurd notion that the two are therefore equals?

Atkinson and Heath (1990) suggest that a shift in personal epistemology is required in order to come to terms with this circular view which suggests that the individual as a part cannot control the whole, and that attempts to do so will lead to pathology at a higher order of the system. They suggest that such a shift in epistemology leads to a view of the world which emphasises its connectedness. They focus on the issue of wilfulness and the damage that this creates in relationships. They suggest that, in family therapy, the issue is not the approach of the therapist but the need of therapists to have clients accept their ideas. What distinguishes a linear approach (1990):

> is not necessarily how directive or non-directive, active or passive, instrumental or non-instrumental, judgmental or non-judgmental the therapist appears to be; it is more related to the extent to which the therapist is determined to have clients accept ideas or suggestions the therapist proposes.

Bateson does not give any clear guidance about how to identify or respond to injustice within a systems framework. He does make it abundantly clear that analysis using the concept of power is counterproductive and will lead to greater problems. This does not mean that Bateson was not passionate in attacking injustice. His criticism of power is that it is a false epistemology and that its use will cause more problems, not less. This section will provide a framework for addressing ethical issues and moral judgements which fits with a systems approach.

Before leaving the concept of power it is worth repeating Bateson's position in one of his clearest statements on the subject (1980):

> It is not so much 'power' that corrupts as the myth of 'power'. It was noted above that 'power', like 'energy', 'tension', and the rest of the quasi-physical metaphors are to be distrusted and, amongst them, 'power' is the most dangerous. He who covets a mythical abstraction must always be insatiable! … we should not promote that myth.

It is necessary to consider more recent developments in systems theory based on the work of Humberto Maturana. Maturana sees the basis for our ethical concerns as being concern for the consequences of behaviour on other people. The recognition that something is unethical is based on emotions (1988): 'What determines whether we see a given behaviour as unethical, and that we act accordingly, is an emotion – love, mutual acceptance, empathy – and not reason.' Maturana goes on to suggest that the ability to recognise ethical concerns is mediated through participation in cultures (local epistemologies) both at the macro and micro level. There is no single standard for ethical behaviour, and an individual's ethical concerns may change as she moves from one local epistemology to another. There are a number of implications of these views about power and abuse for the development of a systems approach. The systems approach cannot be built on the use of power either as a basis for analysis or through the use of 'social authority'. This is because applying concepts of power is seen to corrupt and lead to solutions that fall within the same frame as the problem. Maturana stresses the view that the recognition of abuse and oppression is grounded on emotions and not rationality. There can be no simple definition of what is oppressive or abusive, and an individual social worker or manager may be unable to see the abuse or oppression because of the limitations of their epistemological framework.

Rejecting the use of the metaphor of power does not mean that it is impossible to make moral judgements or that injustice and oppression can be ignored. The ecological view of ethics stresses the role of emotions and particularly empathy for the humanity of others as the basis for ethical action. Maturana states (Krüll, Luhmann and Maturana 1989): 'all our actions against abuse, or against what we call violation of human rights, have an emotional fundament, that supports our rational justification: human empathy.' At the same time Maturana suggests that we frequently write off our emotions and justify our actions rationally.

What then are the ethical issues for someone wishing to apply systems ideas in social work? In his strongly argued criticism of the application of constructivist family therapy, Minuchin (1991) points to the way that, whilst government welfare services are nominally based on the idea that they are protective and humane in operation, they often 'punish, isolate, dismember and humiliate families'. In such situations, he asks, how can it be good to focus solely on the family's narratives and metaphors when their experience is of powerful forces beyond their control shaking and shaping their lives? Whilst Minuchin uses this argument to attack constructivist approaches, it is equally applicable to his own approach to families, which also focuses on processes which occur within families.

It is this issue of the need to widen the target for intervention beyond families and into management and change in social work systems that is at the root of the writers' proposal of a systems approach. In social work the services provided can, as Minuchin has suggested, be punitive and oppressive. At the same time the operation of the social work organisation can similarly be oppressive for its own employees. Third, the organisation is part of a wider system which may be oppressive. For example, a probation service might treat its own staff and its service users in a humane fashion whilst its actions promote the operation of a justice system which is inhumane and oppressive. It can be seen that there are a number of ways in which a social work organisation might provide the worker or manager with ethical dilemmas. Common to all of these is a failure of human empathy, and systems theory proposes that this stems from the particular epistemology within which the oppressor is operating, and which allows the oppressor either not to see the oppression or to rationalise it away.

In looking at issues of oppression, a number of levels need to be considered. To do this it is necessary to adopt a position which enables the user of the systems approach to reflect on issues at any of these levels whether within a family, helping agency or the wider society. This implies a need to consider the different interactions which make up the problem behaviour. It is important to reflect on the nature of these interactions, the language and metaphors used, who participates in them, the actions that these interactions lead to and also their logic, as this gives pointers to the values that they promote. In addition, the user of a systems approach must be open to, and reflect upon, their own feelings and those of others involved in interaction about the problem.

In particular, the viewpoint taken must be considered and its epistemological basis. The person using the systems approach needs to reflect on a wide range of issues. The dangers in this are, on the one hand, that it is easy to think too narrowly and only focus on issues within the organisation, or, on the other hand, to become paralysed by the ever wider and deeper complexity of the problems to be addressed.

For example, in considering the operation of the probation service providing reports to the courts, the interactions to be considered include those in and between the following groups: the offenders; their families and communities; their victims; the probation teams who provided the services; the probation service managers; other agencies involved in the justice system including the police, magistrates and judges, solicitors, etc.; as well as wider societal conversations including those in laws, the press and so on. The idea of the systems approach is to reflect on the place of social work problems within this wider context rather than to attempt to solve all of the problems at all the levels. No consideration of the range of contexts is complete or independent of the worker's own epistemological domain, but considering the wider issues and listening to different ways in which the problem might be described helps the social worker to reflect on the problem in novel ways and to avoid being too 'sucked into' the viewpoint of any one party or group involved with the problem.

Having identified any areas of abuse or oppression, a number of issues need to be considered. The first is that where the social worker or manager feels that the actions of a group are unethical, his/her actions need to enable members of the group to reflect on the consequences of these actions. Attempting to do this by a logical argument, which boils down to telling them that the world is not the way they see it, is likely to lead to anger and rejection. Maturana suggests that what allows us to mistreat others is identifying them as outsiders who are not the subject of mutual concern, and that this is done through conversations of characterisation. A way needs to be found to help those involved in abusive actions to stop or change these conversations. To halt conversations of characterisation means that the social worker or manager needs to find ways of helping those involved in these conversations to recognise the humanity of those who are being characterised. An interaction which leads to such a change in the pattern of conversations will also lead to a new range of possible actions which will have effects on the problem.

Thus a key aspect of the approach is the need to select appropriate systems which are in need of change. For example, in Minuchin's 1991 article discussed above, he describes a situation in which he became involved in working with a mother whose children had been removed from her through court processes which, with the help of psychiatrist's reports, had characterised her as a poor mother. His response was not to try to provide family therapy, but to go with the mother to court and to use his status as a psychologist to help her to get her children back. Thus his target for change was the court which, through its characterisation of her, had split this woman from her children. Whilst the user of the systems approach should have similarly targeted the individual woman's situation, the social worker or manager is also encouraged to look for ways of identifying whether the particular social work organisation had a pattern of similar interactions and, if so, for ways of interacting with it that would create new patterns in which such characterisations did not occur. Through such interventions the systems approach would seek to challenge the oppressive actions of the system as a whole and not just the individual situation. Failure to consider the wider systems can lead to a 'finger in the dike' approach in which individual situations are dealt with whilst an unrecognised pattern of abuse and oppression continues at a different level of the system. Another problem is that these wider systems may undermine or destroy any changes being attempted for individuals.

The systems approach stresses the need to promote cooperation, mutual respect and justice and not to rationalise away feelings of empathy for others. In dealing with problems this requires awareness of one's feelings about one's own actions and those of others both inside and beyond the organisation and, particularly, the implications of these actions for stakeholders. Sensitivity to these emotions will help the social worker or manager to consider the ethics of his/her involvement. It is necessary to consider the wider implications of actions and to avoid the danger that, in tackling an individual's problem or one within an organisation, the changes lead to hubris which can lead to tensions and conflict both within social work organisations, with service users and in the wider ecology of social work. For example, the writers are aware of a number of social services teams which adopted the view that community-based treatment was the best response to offending, and subsequently characterised themselves as the rescuers of young people who were oppressed by the other agencies (police and magistrates). Rather than their approach reducing the use of custody and promoting new ways of responding to young people, their certainty and characterisation of the other agencies led to a hardening of attitudes and harsher treatment. This is not to say that conflicts and tensions can or should be avoided, but that ethical actions should, in the long term, be aimed at reducing abuse by widening cooperation and acceptance of others, rather than by creating an organisation in which individuals feel smug because they see themselves as having found the answers.

Summary

Systems principles drawn from Bateson and other systems writers' work are described not as firm guidelines about what to do with clients in certain situations, but as a way of looking at social work which can help redefine the nature of social work intervention. These principles underpin the chapters that follow on the work with families, individuals and within organisations and are the basis for an ecology of practice in social work.

Circularity

This concept denies a cause-and-effect relationship between events and behaviour in social systems. In social work this means that clients' problems are maintained by current interactions with their social system and that the actions of the social worker and his/her agency have to be considered as possibly maintaining the problems.

Information

This is the key concept drawn from Bateson's work as information is 'the news of difference that makes a difference'. Information is the currency of interaction and is vital if social systems are to survive and change.

Epistemology

This principle relates to the idea that there is no objective experience but that the perceptions we have about our experience define the way we behave and act.

Pattern and form

This is the systems notion that pattern and form in living things are crucial, rather than quantity and logic. The interconnected nature of social systems have to be understood as wholes rather than analysed through the splitting up of the component parts of any system.

Logical types

This deals with the differences between the names of things and the things in themselves and relates to the theory of logical types. It is suggested that it is important to make a distinction between the name of something and the thing in itself in social work if social workers and their managers are to understand systems ideas and to apply them in practice.

Change and stability in social systems

Concepts of change and stability in systems are briefly outlined here in order to explain how social systems deal with new inputs (such as social work help to a family, or a new social work service being introduced within an agency to achieve particular social work tasks).

Power and ethics

This principle relates to the 'myth' of power which is essentially a corrupting notion. An approach based on ethics rather than power is proposed here, which respects and adheres to moral principles and actions.

CHAPTER 3

The Application of Bateson's Ideas in Family Therapy and Wider Systems

> There is a cute story going round about Picasso. A gent wanted him to paint things in a more representational manner. 'Like this photograph of my wife. It is really like her.' Picasso looked at it and said, 'she is small, isn't she, and flat?'
>
> Bateson, *'Afterword' (1977)*

This chapter looks at the development of Bateson's ideas in family therapy. The early approaches were particularly influenced by Bateson's study of schizophrenic communication in families and the idea of double binds. These approaches were based on the idea of therapeutic paradox. Later writing rejected this approach to family therapy and is based on the idea of families as networks of conversations. In recent years this development has included a broadening of the focus of family therapy from families to wider systems.

Systems approaches in family therapy are generally thought to have begun in the 1950s (Hoffman 1981; Walrond-Skinner 1981). Early work was based on such sources as general systems theory, cybernetics and communication theory. Theoreticians and practitioners started to view the family as a 'system' whose parts interacted and evolved, and concepts such as homeostasis and feedback started to be used to understand symptomatic behaviour. There was a rapid development of a wide range of theoretical and practice orientations with no agreement on a core theory or definition of family therapy (Hoffman and Long 1969). At the same time the development of new ideas in cybernetics became quickly integrated into family therapy theory and, for example, the 1960s saw ideas from such authors as Maruyama (1968) moving the theory beyond the initial machine metaphors which had been the result of the application of early cybernetic ideas.

The developments in family therapy which are relevant to this book began in the late 1960s when Bateson's work started to have a major impact on family therapy. At this time his work was being turned into practice models, most notably by the team of Selvini-Palazzoli, Boscolo, Cecchin and Prata in Milan (Selvini-Palazzoli *et al.* 1978, 1980a, 1980b). This team created an approach based on Bateson's ideas of circular causation and the use of therapeutic paradox. At the same time Paul Watzlawick of the Mental Research Institute was considering Bateson's idea that any sequence of events could be understood in a variety of different ways and that the different 'punctuation' of these events was a key element of problems of communication. Watzlawick's influential work at the Family Research Institute continued in the development of brief family therapy (Watzlawick and Weakland 1977) and particularly in his work on therapeutic paradox (Watzlawick *et al.* 1974).

Since that time a number of debates and developments have occurred. These include the move to dealing with wider systems than the family (for an overview see Bilson 1996). There was also a debate about the ethics of family therapy approaches and other implications of the adoption of Bateson's ideas including the development of new practices (again, see Bilson 1996 for an overview), key aspects of which are discussed in the following sections.

The rest of this chapter will provide a selective review of these developments in family therapy identifying key issues relevant to the application of Bateson's work in social work.

Reframing

During the 1970s Paul Watzlawick was developing therapeutic practices in his work at the Mental Research Institute. In *The Language of Change* (1978) he attempted to provide a description of an approach to therapy based on the use of therapeutic paradox. Whilst this is now the subject of critical debate because of its seemingly manipulative nature, there are two major elements which are fundamental in family therapy. These are the use of reframing and his emphasis on language and metaphor.

Watzlawick's approach, reframing (described by a number of authors including Minuchin 1974; Haley 1981; Bandler and Grinder 1982; Cade 1986), has influenced authors in the organisational literature (e.g.

Johannessen 1991; Morgan 1993; Tsouskas 1992) as well as in family therapy. Watzlawick *et al.* (1974) describe reframing as follows:

> To reframe, then, means to change the conceptual and/or emotional setting or viewpoint in relation to which a situation is experienced and to place it in a different frame which fits the 'facts' of the same concrete situation equally well or even better, and thereby changes its entire meaning.

Examples of reframing occur regularly in everyday life – a model can be 'skinny' or 'svelte', a child's behaviour can be described as 'energetic' or 'hyperactive', or life can be a series of adventures or, to quote Lord Peter Wimsey, 'Just one damn thing after another'. Bandler and Grinder (1982) suggest that reframes can focus either on meanings or on contexts.

Virginia Satir (1964) gives an example of a context reframe in her work with a family in which the father, a banker, complained of his daughter's stubbornness. Satir reframed this behaviour by suggesting that he had taught his daughter a lesson that would prove valuable to her in future business situations where tenacity is a valuable personal asset, and that indeed her stubbornness might protect her from unwanted amorous advances. This reframe did not attempt to change the father's view of his daughter's behaviour as being stubborn, but instead suggested that this behaviour in other contexts might be considered a valuable asset.

An example of a meaning reframe is given by Bandler and Grinder (1982). A man was complaining about his wife taking forever to decide on things. He said that when buying clothes she would have to look in every dress shop and view all the clothes before she could decide. They reframed this by saying 'So she is very careful about decisions. Is it not a tremendous compliment that, out of all the men in the world she chose you?' The reframe thus changes the meaning by changing the emotional context, linking the wife's careful decision making to her choice of him as a partner.

Reframing is thus a technique aimed at attempting to change the rational domain within which a problem is being maintained in order to allow those involved to see the possibility of new actions and possible solutions. However, any attempt at reframing needs to take into account the 'views, expectations, reasons, premises – in short the conceptual framework – of those whose problems are to be changed' (Watzlawick *et al.* 1974). The centrality of reframing to attempts to bring about change in therapy continues to be discussed and debated.

Language and metaphor

Watzlawick stresses the importance of listening to the language and metaphors that people use. He sees this as being an essential element in understanding the 'client's values, expectations, hopes, fears, prejudices – in short his world image – as quickly and completely as possible' (Watzlawick 1978). He stresses the importance of listening to the actual words used as well as the metaphors that the speaker employs: 'he [the therapist] also pays attention to the *actual* language of his client and utilises it in his own verbalisations'. He suggests that bringing about change in a world image is facilitated if new ideas are introduced using terms and metaphors which have resonance with those used by the client. Watzlawick is stressing the way that problems are maintained through language and beliefs and that the judicious use of language, metaphors and reframing can change the beliefs and resolve problems.

Within the organisational literature Morgan has based much of his work on Bateson and Watzlawick. He has developed an approach to dealing with problems and change which he calls 'Imaginisation' (Morgan 1986). This combines Batesonian ideas within a postmodern framework. Imaginisation is based on the metaphor of social reality as a text. Drawing on the work of Derrida (1978), he suggests that organisational realities can be considered as living texts which are continually being 'written' and 'read'. His basic idea is that metaphors can help people in organisations to write and read their organisations in new and different ways. He invites (1993) 'you to become your own theorist, using images and metaphors to engage in a continuous construction and deconstruction of meaning in your encounters with everyday reality'.

He thus suggests that new ways of reading the organisation can lead to its transformation and new ways of writing it. Each organisation can be read in a variety of ways which depend on the range of assumptions and perspectives that the reader brings. Imaginisation is intended to help people to become and remain open to the possibility of many different interpretations and hence meanings in any situation, and suggests that such a position leads to new writing of the organisations in ways which are more flexible and adaptable to change.

Circularity

Another influential group of family therapists who have looked at the wider development of Bateson's ideas are the Milan school. Mara Selvini-Palazzoli and her colleagues Luigi Boscolo, Gianfranco Cecchin and Guiliana Prata developed models of family therapy based on Bateson's, as well as on Haley's and Watzlawick's work. Their book *Paradox and Counterparadox* (1980a) covered the development of their approach to working with families with a schizophrenic or psychotic member. In this work they started to recognise the need to consider the wider systems in which their families were involved and in particular the part played by the referring agents. Selvini-Palazzoli has also worked with a group of psychologists providing consultancy to organisations (Selvini-Palazzoli *et al.* 1986) and Cecchin has done much consultation to teams of family therapists and in this way has also applied the ideas beyond family groups.

The work of the Milan school has been summarised by a number of authors (Hoffman 1981; Campbell and Draper 1985; Keeney and Ross 1985; Ross 1987) and it is not intended to describe it extensively here. Central to their early theoretical approach are their guidelines for practice – hypothesising, circularity and neutrality (Selvini-Palazzoli *et al.* 1980a). Cecchin has continued to develop these guidelines within the framework of recent debates about therapeutic approaches (Cecchin 1987).

The Milan team describe hypothesising as the process in which they create a systemic hypothesis which must 'include all components of the family, and must furnish us with a supposition concerning the total relational function' (Selvini-Palazzoli *et al.* 1980a). The main function of the hypothesis is to guide the actions of the interviewer and help to introduce 'the powerful input of the *unexpected* and the *improbable* into the family system' by stopping the interviewer becoming involved in the family's linear view, which is aimed at 'designating who is "crazy" and who is "guilty"' (quotation marks added for emphasis) . Whilst in their early article the Milan school talk of a hypothesis being confirmed or refuted, they also say that it 'is neither true nor false, but rather *more* or *less useful*'. In a more recent article, Cecchin makes the issue of the validity of the hypothesis clearer. He suggests that the move to hypothesising by the Milan group was a move away from the certainty and truth of explanations. Thus he states (1992):

> It took us some time to find out that it was not the quality of our hypothesis that made a difference. Rather, the difference was made by the contrast (the relationship) between our hypothesis and the family's or between the different hypotheses that emerged during the conversation.

In a single example of such a hypothesis Selvini-Palazzoli *et al.* describe an interview with a divorced mother and adolescent son. They came for therapy because of constant fights. The first hypothesis of the team was that the boy's behaviour might, in part, be a disguised attempt to bring the natural father back to the family home. During the process of circular questioning that hypothesis came to be seen as unlikely, given the answers and reactions of mother and son. A new hypothesis was developed. The mother had seriously begun dating another man for the first time in the 12 years since the divorce. The son was at the age of seeking more freedom. The mother–son couple was beginning to break up and the conflicting systems issue – that of changing and staying the same – created a systems dilemma which their continuous fights 'solved'. They could stay together whilst fighting to be apart. The team's hypothesis was that they were unavoidably growing apart and the team's intervention was that the couple come to see them, not for therapy but for a few meetings 'to try to slow down this painful process of separation'.

The systemic hypothesis allows for the collection of data and the development of an intervention and is not viewed as the 'ultimate truth'. There are, in systems terms, as many versions of the truth about a family as there are people to observe it. Inevitably, there is a distorting linear form to any hypothesis. In the example given above, Selvini-Palazzoli *et al.* describe the interactional behaviour of the system by saying that the mother's relationship with another man leads to her moving further from her son. One could describe the same scenario by saying that her son's new friends and maturity led her to seek a new relationship which led him to seek other relationships and so on, *ad infinitum.* Each of these descriptions 'punctuate' the same pattern of interactions differently and whilst some descriptions fit better than others they do not represent 'truths'.

The second guideline, circularity, explicitly related their approach to the theories of Bateson on circular causation. They suggest two fundamentals to the idea of circularity. These are that 'information is a difference' and that 'difference is a relationship' (1980a). They developed a form of interviewing known as circular questioning. In this approach a member of the family is asked to comment on the relationship between two other members in their presence. A number of specific types of question were described.

Cecchin suggests that the aim of circular questioning is to disrupt the family's belief systems in ways which create opportunities for new stories (1987):

> Circular questions undermine the family's belief system by using the language of relationship, not of 'what is.' This may be done by 'if'

> questions and by future oriented questions (for example 'If your mother decided to stop worrying about you, what would your father do?'). These questions imply patterns not facts. The moment a question undermines the belief system, it creates opportunities for new stories.

A key issue in the use of circular questions is that they are asked in the presence of the family members as a whole. The information gained from them is not simply the answers that are given but, more importantly, the verbal and non-verbal responses of the people to whom the answer relates. Thus in the example in the quote above the mother's and father's responses to the question would be a major source of information about their relationship both for the therapist and for family members.

The third guideline, neutrality, is the one which has caused most controversy and criticism. In the original article that proposed neutrality it was suggested that the more familiar the interviewer becomes with a systems approach the less they will 'make moral judgements' (1980a). The Milan school adopted this approach because they felt that expressions of approval or disapproval inevitably led to an alliance with one of the family members which meant that the interviewer became unable to see circular causal patterns. Thus neutrality was not meant to imply objectivity, but to be an approach which reduced the chance of getting involved in the family game which was the reason for referral and caused the family's pain. Thus Cecchin (1987) states: 'Accepting our inability to act in neutral or non-political ways, the term "neutrality" was originally used to express the idea of actively avoiding the acceptance of any one position as more correct than another.' Cecchin goes on to suggest that neutrality is about trying to see patterns rather than to adopt linear causal explanations. The criticism of this approach has been that it is morally relativist and is unable to allocate responsibility where there is abuse of power or violence.

The final element of the Milan team's approach is their use of paradox. The key aspect of this is a form of symptom prescription[1] which they call positive connotation. Positive connotation was often used at the end of a session. Symptom prescriptions had been used in strategic therapy for some

1 Symptom prescription is used in a range of therapies. It consists of asking someone to increase the behaviour that has brought them to therapy. A commonly known example is used in sex counselling where couples who have problems in making love are asked to refrain from the act of intercourse whilst it is suggested that they should enjoy each other's bodies and engage in foreplay. The frequent result of this paradoxical request is that the problem of love making disappears.

time. The Milan school found that in asking a family to maintain or increase its symptomatic behaviour they simply moved from focusing on the identified patient to blame others, usually the parents. They saw this as joining the family game and felt that it prevented them from taking a circular causal view. In order to use symptom prescription in a circular causal framework they prescribe the symptom whilst giving a positive explanation of the need for all the members of the family to maintain the behaviours involved in the symptom. The use of positive connotation has now largely been abandoned by writers on the Milan approach, whilst circular questioning is still seen as an important tool and is used or referred to by a number of current authors on family therapy (Cade 1982; McNamee 1992).

The key aspects of the application of Bateson's concept of circularity in the work of the Milan school and many thereafter is the acceptance that causal chains are not linear and with this the rejection of the search for root causes of problems. This was combined with an approach to interviewing which created information by highlighting differences in opinions, beliefs and so on.

Circularity in wider systems

The idea of circularity has also been used in applications of family therapy techniques to wider systems such as organisations. Imber-Black (1986b, 1988) is influenced by circular questioning in her description of three areas which she sees as being necessary to explore when carrying out a consultancy in human service provider organisations. She uses circular questioning techniques to clarify these areas, asking members of the organisation to comment on the actions or relationships of others who are normally also present.

Williams (1989), drawing on the Milan model, writes about the 'problem' of the referring person. He points out that the consultant needs to join with the whole organisation, not a part of it, and that, whilst referring is not a crime, it is a crucial part of the consultant's initial investigation to assess 'the special status of the referring person' (1989). Williams suggests that the neutrality of the consultant can be affected by two types of bias. One is the bias towards a particular person or subgroup of those in the organisation (this being what would normally be understood by the term bias). The other form of bias is towards the way that the organisation as a whole formulates and understands the problem. In this second form of bias the consultant is pulled into the system, adopting its epistemology or world view, and hence its view of the problem and the range of possible solutions. Williams calls this latter form of bias 'canonisation' because it leads the consultant into thinking in the same way about the problem as the members of the system and setting a seal of approval on the system's thinking.

As an example of canonisation Williams discusses an organisation which has approached the consultant because it has problems with communication. He points out that a consultant who accepts this definition of the problem may then attempt to get members of the organisation to communicate better. However, it is likely that the attempted solutions of an organisation in such a situation have been to get better communications, and in attempting to get them to be better still the consultant is joining the organisational game – in Watzlawick *et al.*'s (1974) terms, entering a 'more of the same' loop.

Thus a number of family therapists have attempted to apply insights from their practice with families to the organisational setting. In the main these attempts have been limited to providing consultancy for teams which have themselves been practising family therapy.

Problem-determined systems

Along with these specific attempts to apply family therapy approaches to organisations and other 'systems', a further development has been to consider that systems are not defined by concepts such as family or team but to think of them as networks of people in conversation. A conversation in this sense does not just consist of the verbal statements but of the complicated network of verbal and non-verbal interactions and behaviours. A specific and useful idea in this area is the problem-determined system.

The idea of problem-determined systems comes from Harlene Anderson and Harold Goolishian's understandings of the ideas of Bateson. These ideas have led to what has been called by Hoffman the 'new epistemology'. The notion is that the system which needs to be worked with is the set of people who are creating the network of conversations about the problem. Goolishian and Winderman define a problem-determined system as follows (1988):

> We are attempting to move beyond systems that are predefined on the basis of traditional, customary social definition. Thus, we abandon treatment models defined by such concepts as individual, marital couple, family and larger social system. We define the treatment system on the basis of those who are actively engaged in linguistic interaction ... vis-à-vis a problem ... We call the treatment system defined in this manner a Problem Determined System.

In this position there is a shift from viewing systems as creating problems to viewing them as arising because of conversations about the problem. Goolishian and Winderman go on to state that 'systems do not make problems; languaging about problems makes systems'. The implication of this is that the problem-determined system consists of the individuals who are actively and repeatedly participating in the network of interactions about the problem. Immediately a referral takes place this includes not only the systems practitioners but also the referring person if he/she has a significant part in the network. This does not mean that, in order to deal with a problem-determined system, the whole of the system needs to be assembled or that practice must directly involve everyone at all times; but rather that in thinking about a problem, this wider context of the problem-determined system needs to be considered. The idea of a problem-determined system does not mean that there is a consensus about the nature and meaning of the problem. In fact, the system will include a range of different understandings and meanings of the problem.

The task of someone working in this framework is to manage a conversation that is respectful of these multiple views of the problem. He/she guides the conversation, not towards a particular goal but rather in a way which opens the possibility of new meanings (1988): 'The therapist's skill lies in his or her finely tuned sensitivity to language, and the ability to ask questions which open the conversation to the elaboration of new meanings and communicative connections.' An important principle is that the therapy is not seen to be working towards a predefined goal or end, but rather that new meanings will develop. Goolishian thus suggests that 'Treatment is the process of dis-solving (in a sense, unsolving fixed meanings) a problem system, rather than finding solutions for problems'. This principle of not working towards a particular outcome or solution is central to the approaches which use the metaphor of the conversation.

Goolishian and Winderman thus put together a framework for therapy that carefully avoids a normative approach, having no ideal states towards which the problem-determined system is aimed, but only an emphasis on moving away from pain through an accepting and unstructured conversation. Their definition of the system as being the set of people in conversation about the problem moves their approach away from the usual focus on the family and this makes it a useful way of viewing problems in a range of contexts.

Reflexive conversations

The reflecting team is Tom Anderson's (1991, 1992) contribution to the concept of therapy as a conversational art. Amongst the basic concepts of this approach is Bateson's idea of 'news of difference that makes a difference'. In practice, this approach has tried to deal with an imbalance of power between the family therapy team and families. A key difference from previous family therapy approaches is that instead of the interviewer meeting privately to discuss the family with the consulting team who have observed the interview, usually from behind a one-way screen, this process is changed and the team have their conversation about what they have seen and understood about the interview watched by the family. This is, in turn, followed by the family reflecting on the conversation of the team. Thus this approach has brought the family therapy team out from behind its one-way screen and into a more 'equal' interaction with the family.

The idea behind this approach is that in these conversations, reflections on conversations and reflections on reflections, a space will be generated in which the system being worked with can develop new and different meanings. The person interviewing the family attempts to ask questions which are unusual, but not too unusual. Anderson states that questions that are 'too unusual' will make no difference nor offer new perspectives, because the family will become closed to the process of the interview. If questions are 'too unusual' the participants 'listen less attentively, become distant and uninterested, their answers are shorter and fewer' (1991). The types of questions used in a reflecting team interview are similar to those used in circular questioning.

During the interview the reflecting team sit in silence, listening to their own internal dialogues and their emotional responses in order not to lose possible descriptions through discussions. They then talk, usually for about five to ten minutes, whilst the family listen. The rules of this conversation are that there should be no negative connotations and no reference to things not pertaining to the conversation seen. The manner of these reflections is tentative, in recognition of the many possible versions of the issues dealt with. The reflection stresses complementarity, taking a both/and position rather than stressing one particular view – 'in addition … both this can be seen and this …', and so forth. The reflexive conversation allows members of the system to discuss their own discussions and in this reflexive process comes the possibility of identifying patterns in previous interactions and creating new possibilities.

One of the claims about this approach is that it deals more effectively with issues of power. Although families do get to see what is said about them by the consulting team this does not equalise power. It is still the therapists that make the rules, that are being paid, that have the status and so on. However, the idea of reflecting on conversations within systems is a very important one. The framework of having the members of the system speak and then listen to reflections on that from outside and finally discussing these reflections can be adapted to be used outside the privileged atmosphere of the consulting rooms with their one-way mirrors, for example social work colleagues, even if doing interviews in a family home, can use the basic structure. The key aspect of a reflexive conversation is finding ways to enable the members of the system to reflect on and expand or change the assumptions and values of their epistemological framework and not some particular mode of interviewing.

Who's afraid?

An example of social work using an approach based on these family therapy approaches occurred in our work with a young widow with two boys aged six and four who came complaining of the disturbed behaviour of the six-year-old. The boy refused to go to bed at night and had temper tantrums when confronted by the mother. The following hypothesis was constructed from the data given by the family. The boy's behaviour was linked to a stress point in the family's lifecycle, perhaps specifically to the mother's attempt to get over the death of her husband and move back into a normal lifestyle. It emerged from interviewing the family that the boy was of the view that there were wolves in the ceiling of his room that looked in on him at night and that for over eighteen months since his father's death, despite repeated attempts by his mother to reassure him, he had been in the habit of sleeping with his mother in her bed. Recently, however, the mother had started dating a new man and occasionally he stayed the night. On these occasions the boy slept in the hallway, often with his brother, who could vouch for the presence of wolves in the subject's bedroom.

In conversation with the family it was suggested that the boy, being so sensitive and caring about his mother's feelings, realised that she might well think it was appropriate to try and pick up a new life. However, he knew how much the tragic death of his father had hurt her and he had to remind her constantly that for their family there were 'wolves' (or bad things) outside waiting for them if they should try to venture out into a new life. He had decided to help his brother and mother by reminding them that they could not afford to let down their guard. When the family were seen again, three weeks after this prescription was given, the mother had returned both children to their own bedrooms without any difficulties and had moved on in the session to describe her concerns about how she would explain her new relationship to her parents, who were shortly to visit her.

This example shows how the metaphors used by members of the system are an important indicator of the nature of the problem and of the need for the user of a systems approach to be sensitive to the way that the system communicates about its problems. Similarly, the reframing of the situation offered in the conversation with the family provided a new and positive way of understanding the boy's behaviour. The conversation was reflective in that it encouraged the family to reflect on the patterns of its previous interactions and from the conversation it appears that new meaning was developed.

Summary

This chapter has examined development in the field of family therapy from approaches based on a Batesonian epistemology. It has shown how family therapists have developed ways of working with families which have developed not only new metaphors for systems but also new practical approaches to bring about change in a range of situations. The range and diversity of these approaches demonstrates that adopting a systems approach does not lead to any single or unified model of practice. Rather it challenges professional certainties. These approaches have in common the idea that problems are maintained by our conversations about the problem and that the task of someone working with a problem is to generate new conversations that 'make a difference'. Another common feature is the need to join the conversations by not being 'too unusual' and matching the language and metaphors used by the problem-determined system in their conversations about the problem. They also indicate the need to move from normative models of problems and their solutions to a position in which the actions of the social worker or manager help the problem to dissolve.

Whilst Bateson did not see his research as providing models for practice or developing taxonomies of how one might intervene with families with certain problems, his analysis of the nature of interaction and change was fundamental to how these therapists conceptualised and carried out their work.

The chapter has briefly described a range of attempts to apply Batesonian ideas to the practice of family therapy as well as to problems in other contexts. It highlights the following features of practice and explains why these are relevant in a systems framework.

Reframing

Reframing is a technique aimed at attempting to change the rational domain within which a problem is being maintained in order to allow those involved to see the possibility of new actions and possible solutions. A reframe needs to take into account the 'views, expectations, reasons, premises – in short the conceptual framework – of those whose problems are to be changed' (Watzlawick *et al.*). Many authors still see reframing as being the major approach to change in therapy.

Language and metaphor

This section stresses the importance of listening to the actual words used as well as the metaphors that the speaker employs. Changes in epistemology can be promoted if new ideas are introduced using terms and metaphors which have resonance with those used by those within the system.

Circularity

The key aspects of the application of Bateson's concept of circularity in the work of the Milan school and many thereafter was the acceptance that causal chains are not linear and with this the rejection of the search for root causes of problems. This has been combined with an approach to interviewing which created information by highlighting differences in opinions, beliefs and so on.

Problem-determined systems

The definition of the system as being the set of people in conversation about the problem moves away from the usual focus on the family and provides a useful way of viewing problems in a range of contexts. This framework carefully avoids a normative approach, having no ideal states towards which the problem-determined system is aimed, but only an emphasis on moving away from pain through an accepting and unstructured conversation.

Reflexive conversations

The key aspect of a reflexive conversation is finding ways to enable the members of the problem-determined system to reflect on and expand or change the assumptions and values of their epistemological framework.

CHAPTER 4

Towards an Ecology of Social Work Practice

> And then what you need to do is to try to do something that induces a change in the patient – any little change. Because the patient wants a change, however small, and he will accept that as a change and then follow that change and the change will develop in accordance with his own change and in accordance with his own needs. It's much like rolling a snowball down a mountainside. It starts out a small snowball, but as it rolls down it gets larger and larger ... and starts an avalanche that fits to the shape of the mountain.
>
> Milton H. Erickson, Personal Communication (1977)

An 'ecology' of practice starts from the premise that natural systems are capable of stability and change and have an order and responsiveness to new circumstances which ensures their continuation over time. The description of the 'deep water dilemma for Falmouth' in the first chapter described how the intervention of human beings into a natural system to try to bring new work into Falmouth would have consequences throughout the eco-system. It would have an impact on animal and plant life, on the people who live in the area, and on tourists who may choose not to visit it any more; indeed it would affect all aspects of life there. The same phenomenon can be identified in social work practice. For example a child's removal from home (what Haley (1980a) calls 'a parentectomy') as a result of committing offences or because of risk of injury, affects the total family and community system of which he/she is a part. Ultimately, what Bateson calls the 'self-healing tautological properties' of the family system deal with the removal of one element by 'closing off' the child's place so they no longer belong in the family. Thus the rehabilitation of the child and family becomes perilously difficult to achieve. But the child's removal also has consequences on a wider circle than that of the family. It affects the community's and indeed ultimately society's ways of dealing with crime and deviance. Offending in children becomes identified as something for social workers, police, psychologists and so on to deal with, rather than behaviour associated with childhood which can be dealt with by informal, non-statutory methods. The ripples of the action of removal spread out very much more widely than the impact on the individual.

A social worker with a systems perspective will affect the 'eco-system' of their client and the effect will be felt within the client's family and community – their 'natural system'. An example of this from the writers' experience occurred when a young boy, David, attended a group because he exhibited violent behaviour towards a teacher and was said to be 'a very disturbed child'. He made good progress in the group and appeared to be learning how to control his temper with other adults and his parents. The group were to spend a few days in the Lake District as part of their 'group experience'. On the afternoon before the group were due to set out for the Lakes, David's headmistress rang the social services department. He had appeared at school with his father's cut-throat razor, had to be taken home and his parents had to be told. A short while later the boy appeared at the social work office with a black eye and bruising on his shoulders and chest saying his father had hit him. When the father was interviewed he acknowledged that he had hit him because he was angry with him, not because of the razor incident, but because he did not see why he should be able to go away 'on holiday' when he and his wife had never been away on holiday in 20 years. He resented his boy getting 'treats' when nothing was ever offered to help him and his wife. This example demonstrates clearly how seeking to bring about a change in one part of a system – here the boy's behaviour – had a clear impact on other parts of the system, his father's behaviour towards him. The intervention, aimed at helping the child, actually 'created' a tension in the relationship between the boy and his father that made the boy's situation worse. The incident at school was a trigger for the boy to be punished by his father but was not its cause.

Social work intervention based on systems principles has to work within the 'ecology' of the client and take the wider systems issues into account. The social worker, therefore, has to 'track' the effects of their interventions with clients throughout the systems of which the client is a part. Just as the family therapists from the Milan school use circular questioning to find out how the problem affects other people in the family and how they seek to maintain it, so too must the social worker obtain information about how other members of a client's system affect, and are affected by, the actions of the client. This moves away from the usual notions of a social work assessment which tends to concentrate on an individual's behaviour and feelings about their situation and into the detailed identification of interactional patterns within the client's system. The social worker and his/her agency have to try to think about the system as a whole – by identifying the key patterns occurring in it, including their own moves in the 'dance' (Minuchin 1974) or problem behaviour – without losing the ability to be involved in and responsive to what is happening to the client. In that sense the social worker has to attempt to do what Castaneda's (1972) sorcerer referred to as 'being outside the circle that presses' their fellow men. This is difficult to achieve and many writers in the family therapy literature and in the literature of social work (Jordan 1981; Walrond-Skinner 1976) talk of the 'suck-in' effect of families once a worker gets involved.

Wynne (1958) calls this phenomenon the 'rubber fence', so that the worker, when trying to introduce new behaviour into a family, is 'bounced back' into the behaviour and beliefs of the family. This effect can only be counteracted by careful and effective consultation and supervision within the agency. The family therapy literature has much to say about the use of live supervision and consultation, using videos and one-way screens to help the therapists stay outside the family system (Haley 1980b; Adler and Levy 1981; Breslin and Cade 1981; Cade and Cornwall 1983). The analysis of pattern is a subjective and partial exercise, since no worker can ever identify all the actions within a system. There are, however, practical ways which can be developed to help attempt this identification of pattern.

In systems terms, the identification of pattern is not a prerequisite for action but an 'intervention' in itself. It is not a scientific exercise observing actual factual data, but a work of art based on the aesthetics of assembling pieces of known behaviour into sequences – trying to create meaning and information from what is 'known' (Bateson 1980). Social workers are involved in the creation of information about their clients through their ability to introduce 'news of difference' between the client's view of their problem and wider views and opinions within their system. They are not analysing 'facts' which are verifiable in some ultimate reality or 'truth'. This has implications for the management and supervision of social work practice as well as for the conception of the nature of the social work task. An assessment of a situation based on the client in context is, in itself, an intervention into a client's life since it creates 'news of difference' and this is information. Every action has an effect within the system – the questions social workers ask, the questions they do not ask, the nature of their interaction, their beliefs about what they observe – all become information for the client and the client-plus-worker and hence for the client's system of which the social worker and his/her agency are a part. Every intervention by the social worker becomes a significant definer of all the possible outcomes for the client's system.

This means that a social worker's actions have to be seen as the important determinant of how a client responds to social work intervention. Social workers who wish to adopt systems principles cannot see themselves as passive reactors to situations, or as impartial observers, responding to the raw data of client actions; they have to see themselves as prime movers and key determinants of how a system will respond. Social workers do not generally see themselves in this way. Jordan and Brandon (1979) described 'most people's stereotype' of a social worker which was 'reflected in the literature of the profession' as:

> a profoundly uncreative being, a passive, reasonable, dull, smiling sponge which soothes troubled surfaces with abundant soft soap: a Uriah Heep figure without the redeeming evil intentions. When new social work students are asked to play the role of a helper, they often produce a performance as narrow and rigid as the most institutionalised client.

Social workers who wish to adopt a systems approach cannot see themselves as passively reacting to their client's problems. However, as can be seen from the example of David quoted earlier, the changes created by social work intervention may not constitute an improvement in the client's situation and may indeed make a client's life worse.

The consequences for practice of such an important issue are not extensively examined in the literature or methodology of social work. If a social worker's actions can actually create more distress and tension for a client then the question has to be asked, is social work, as an activity, nevertheless valid? We would claim that social work practice can be valid but that the only way to handle the dilemma posed by intervention is to pay more attention to the nature of that intervention and to the patterns of behaviour created by the agency's response to clients. This means that instead of assuming that social workers are there to help people in all kinds of human difficulties and that social work must therefore be a good thing, rather, social workers have to be very much more discriminating about circumstances in which they intervene. Many potential clients will sort out their difficulties without help or with very little help from social work agencies. Paul Watzlawick *et al.* in *Change* (1974) talk about the danger of being drawn into a 'Utopian syndrome' where one believes that there are solutions to all life's difficulties (unhappiness, boredom, bereavement, sorrow, grief, anger, etc.) and that this mistaken belief causes social workers to pursue solutions to difficulties that only become problems because of the belief that they should be solved. They quote, for example, the 'generation gap' between parents and their children, which has always existed in families but which only becomes a problem when someone tries to 'solve' it by trying to close it or cure it.

In social work there are many examples of Utopianism, usually resulting in the creation of 'more of the same loops' in which the clients get worse as the social worker continues to try to solve a problem to which there is no realisable solution. As the poet Holdekin remarked 'What has made the State into hell is that man wanted to make it heaven' (in Watzlawick *et al.* 1974). Such Utopianism in social work undermines legitimate roles for social work and damages the lives of those who take part in the attempted solutions.

An example of Utopianism involved an elderly woman who lived alone and had had a stroke which limited her ability to communicate. The woman was lonely, isolated and depressed. The social worker intervened to take her into a residential home because 'The only time Mrs Smith is happy is when in the company of others and residential care could offer her this.' However, on entry to the home the woman was still unable to interact due to her difficulties with speech and a review two months after her entry stated that she 'finds it very difficult to form relationships in her peer group due to her speech defect. When spoken to she will respond with a smile and would love to be able to participate ... she is very self-conscious when she soils herself.' In this case the woman not only had to adapt to a new environment in which she was no less isolated, lonely or depressed, but she had also lost her home and was continually confronted with her inability to communicate or join in.

In another example a social worker who had supervised the placement of a 14-year-old girl and her two brothers in the same foster placement for seven years felt that the foster parents had not come to terms with their own childlessness and that the couple themselves had never really 'worked through' the fact that they could not have children of their own and that the foster children, whom they intended to adopt, were not 'theirs'. The social worker assumed that this was the reason for tension between the children and the foster parents and that, by concentrating on these unresolved issues, the situation for all of them could improve. The results of such an analysis and focus became apparent very quickly. The foster placement became increasingly tense, the foster parents began to doubt their commitment to the children and their ability to parent them and, rather suddenly, the two boys were removed whilst the girl remained, through a dubious decision-making process. At the time of the writers' involvement, the girl's placement was also breaking down. The foster parents were hurt and confused by events. They had now lost two children whom they regarded as their family and were left with a girl who had lost her two brothers and who was waiting for the social worker to remove her too, if the relationship between her and the foster parents became any more strained. All parties doubted their ability to care for each other. The girl occasionally ran away to see her brothers, who were 380 miles away, and her foster parents continually had to decide whether they wished this placement to continue. Their own childlessness had been reinforced by the two children that were removed and about whom they felt guilty. The 'more of the same loop' was evident and the social work task had to be redefined to minimise the ecological disasters to this girl's life and that of her foster parents by helping them accept the inadequacies of their life together rather than looking at what might have been. There was evidence that the social work intervention created an ecological disaster – an intervention based on a Utopian view that their life difficulties (in this case the foster parents' grief for their childlessness) could be solved by social work help. This attempted solution increased the pressure on their system to the point where it began to break up. In a systems approach the broadening of the analysis to include the actions of helping agencies and the identification of patterns of response to attempts to help should reduce the likelihood of Utopianism.

For those clients whose problems are great – those whose behaviour or circumstances are life-threatening or whose situation is such that their system is breaking up, or a family member is facing removal (a person facing a custodial sentence, a young person being rejected and removed from home into residential care, an elderly person facing institutionalisation because of frailty, for example) – then the rationale for intervention must be that the social worker has the resources and skills to make the situation better for the client and the client's system. In a systems approach the social worker must minimise ecological disasters, not create situations which threaten not only the lives of those involved but also of others who are connected with the client's system. There are many important issues in trying to develop an ecology of practice which enables social workers to define a purposeful social work agenda with their clients. The following are guidelines for an ecology of social work, not a model or a set of prescriptive rules. They provide rather a series of principles for practice which, if adopted, will enable social workers to work in an ecological framework with their client and their families. These principles are closely related to those outlined for management and organisational change. They link and overlap in a circular way in that the manager's tasks in social work should help social workers follow these principles in their practice. These principles are:

- creating order
- creative resolution based on minimal intervention
- fit
- reframing
- circularity in social work practice.

Creating order

The fact that, over time, everything turns to disorder (entropy increases) is based upon one of the basic laws of physics (the second law of thermodynamics). This does not occur in living systems. Bateson's notion of a self-healing tautology is, according to Dell, that 'in living interactional systems, order spontaneously arises' (1982). However, the order that arises may be the order of a 'rigid pathological family system' frequently dealt with by social workers. Again, according to Dell (1982):

> Pathological families are full of individuals who repeatedly and determinedly inflict those epistemological errors on themselves and those around them. Because epistemological errors almost always preclude the outcome they were designed to attain, those individuals are forced to keep trying – over and over ... No wonder those families have such rigidly stereotyped patterns of interaction.

When social workers intervene and perturb such a system the likelihood is that the results will not be those expected or sought. However, it is only when interventions fail to resolve the difficulties that most social workers examine what they have been trying to achieve. This examination often results in increased efforts to increase the degree of intervention further. This is 'blunderbuss' social work and its effects are to create ecological disasters in the lives of clients, their families and the community, which can seldom be dealt with except by drastic action (often necessitating the restriction of the civil liberties of a client or his family – by incarceration, removal from society, a restriction of legal rights, etc.).

An example of this involved a 13-year-old boy called Hamish who came to the writers' notice when his foster placement was reported by his social worker to be breaking down. His father was a single parent and was profoundly deaf. He was looking after his four children following his wife's sudden death two years earlier. Hamish had seen his mother die and was referred to in his file as having 'unresolved grief' about his mother's death. He had run away from home a few times and was involved in shoplifting, though was always caught red-handed. The social worker had asked Hamish if he would like to be in a foster home. He had said he was not sure but would give it a try. His father was struggling to look after the children at home and the house was rather dirty and chaotic and, though he was concerned not to lose Hamish, he agreed to a reception into care because he wanted to do the best thing for him. A foster couple were identified who had never fostered before. They were regarded as a good, middle-class family who lived on a farm and, since Hamish liked animals, the placement was established because it would give Hamish 'an idea of fostering' so he 'could decide if he wanted to be fostered'. Then he would be placed with suitable long-term foster parents, once some could be identified. The placement would also give the foster couple some opportunity to try their hand with an adolescent boy who was regarded by the social work department at that time as relatively easy to handle.

After a few weeks the foster parents believed it was going well and Hamish stated he wanted them to be his foster parents in the long term; the foster parents wanted that also. The placement was never intended to be long term, but the social worker and her manager saw no reason to refuse and agreed to maintain the placement. After a few months the foster parents started to get angry with the department because they regarded the financial payments made to foster parents in clothing allowances for children as totally inadequate. They claimed that Hamish 'showed them up' socially because of his clothing. Despite a range of payments for clothing and allowances for Hamish, their dissatisfaction at the local authority's financial arrangements escalated and were given as the reason for their demand, six months later, that Hamish be taken away from them.

Hamish was, by now, behaving in a disturbed way and was stealing small amounts of money from his classmates at school. His father was unsure whether Hamish could come back home because his behaviour had deteriorated over the last few months. In this example there are a range of assumptions about Hamish's behaviour and the action of the foster parents and the social workers. Hamish's removal from home was born of a belief that this boy's difficulties could be solved. This had disastrous outcomes for the child, his family, the foster family and on the social work agency's response to the case, which was now not just that of a deprived child and his handicapped father struggling to survive in the community, but of a disturbed delinquent who needed a special foster placement or residential establishment since he had failed in a foster placement. The 'more of the same' loop was underway with each subsequent action being guided by the failure of the one before, leading to worse and worse outcomes. As Forrester describes (1972): 'Commitment increases to the apparent solution. If the presumed solution actually makes matters worse, the process by which this happens is not evident. So, when the troubles increase, the efforts are intensified that are actually worsening the problem.'

At this stage the whole basis for intervention with Hamish and his family had to be re-evaluated and the child returned home. It is important to note, however, that in returning a child from care in a situation like the one described, the problem definition at the point of removal is usually less serious than at the stage of returning the client after a period in care. The notion of a self-healing tautology would predict that new order would 'spontaneously' occur in the family adjusting to the absence of the removed child.

It is frequently argued that if social workers intervene without purpose or planning it is because of agency pressures – busy offices which have many expectations placed on them, legislation which requires social work responses, elected members who expect local services to be administered in politically popular ways. All these 'excuses' for mindless bureaucratic responses have some degree of fit with the 'realities' of practising social work. Over all these, however, the fact that social work repeatedly fails to develop a consistent view of the nature of the tasks of a social worker results in social work consistently failing to introduce effective 'news of difference' into problematic situations.

The lack of order (structure and pattern) in social worker's interventions leads to a likelihood that randomness and disorder in the client and agency systems will increase. As Keeney says (1983), 'It is only by distinguishing one pattern from another that we are able to know our world' and the key task of a social worker and his/her manager is to identify those situations where people need social work and to relate any intervention to the creation specific beneficial changes. An ecology of social work practice means that, having decided to intervene in a particular situation, a hypothesis has to be formulated about what the problems are and how social work legitimately has a role in improving the situation. In the previous chapter the central role that hypothesising plays in systemic family therapy has been demonstrated. The same applies in systems approaches to social work practice. The process of hypothesising and checking the hypotheses through inputs into the family system not only helps to bring order to the social worker's interaction, but also provides 'news of difference' in the family–social worker system. It enables understanding of how problems are maintained and the role of the social work agency in the maintaining of them.

An example from the writers' practice occurred when the social work department was contacted about a 14-year-old girl who had complained at school of having been beaten by her mother. She had been examined by her teachers and found to have some small bruises on her shoulder. The social work department instigated child abuse procedures, called for a case conference of all agencies and notified the police, who charged the mother with assault. The girl was the oldest of four children and the mother was a single parent who still maintained some contact with the child's father, her former husband. The mother was ambivalent about having her husband back. The assault was sustained following an incident when the girl stayed out late without telling her mother where she was. The girl was also in the habit of associating with a local older and rather disreputable man against her mother's wishes. Her mother had hit out in anger against her when they fought over this.

The following systemic hypothesis was developed. The girl's behaviour was part of a repeating pattern which was functional to all members of the family system. The girl, by refusing to obey her mother, engaged her in a series of complementary escalating manoeuvres (like the vaunting rituals in the 'Naven' ceremony). At the point in their relationship when the system became threatened by such manoeuvres (in systems terms when it was 'going into a runaway') the pattern was that the girl's father got reinvolved. The mother would appeal for his help to control their daughter. His position in the family was temporarily restored and the daughter's behaviour improved.

When the tension between the girl and her mother was eased, her father would leave and the pattern would start again within a few months.

The hypothesis suggested that this pattern had gone on for some time with her behaviour gradually escalating – 'more of the same loop'. Eventually the statutory agencies (what Thorpe calls the 'system definers'), in this case the school and the social work department, became involved. The rows about who had the most power, mother or daughter, escalated to the point where the mother had used force and the daughter, in order to maintain a complementary position, threatened her mother with the 'welfare'. This manoeuvre increased the stakes in terms of threats to the system's survival. Once the school, the social work department and the police came in to protect the girl, her mother, in order to maintain her complementary position, had to reject her daughter more forcibly and state she was 'beyond her control'. This necessitated the involvement of the judicial process, in this case the children's hearings system. The father's reinvolvement, which usually maintained the integrity of the family system, was ineffective in helping the usual response of the system once the other agencies were involved.

The intervention of the social worker and his agency based on this hypothesis was agreed thus – first, the department had to be involved once an injury (although minor) had been sustained by the child from her mother's attempts to control her. The double bind, referred to by Hoffman and Long (1969), that the agency by their involvement further define the family as inadequate was clear and unavoidable. However, the social work response could aim at breaking the pattern by helping the girl's mother to control her child's behaviour without violence and without having to appeal to her ex-husband. Further, in order to minimise the problem raised by Haley that 'any treatment which defines the person as abnormal tends to perpetuate the problem', the intervention was framed as a part of a mother's natural attempts to control her teenage daughter and was thus normalised. This plan reduced the risk that the child would be removed from the family into care where the close relationships between mother and daughter would be harder to sustain, the father's involvement would be impossible and the place that the child had in the family would be changed irrevocably. An agenda for social work was agreed with the mother and daughter in a way that both could understand. The social worker would help the mother to control her daughter's behaviour in acceptable and effective ways which would not harm her.

In systems terms an additional task for the social worker was dealing with the responses of the significant agencies – school, police, children's hearings system and his own social work department, to ensure that there was no over-reaction to the problem. This latter aspect of the work, often referred to as 'systems management' (Thorpe *et al.* 1980), is as important a role for the social worker as face-to-face work with the family. It must be monitored closely through direct supervision, agency reviews and case consultancy so that feedback to the worker about his performance in helping to resolve the problem situation will be a continuous part of the practice.

A similar focused approach of working with young people at risk or in trouble is described by Haley (1980a). He outlines the significance of dealing briefly with the immediate problematic interaction:

> In essence, the therapy approach is like an initiation ceremony. The procedure helps parents and offspring disengage from each other so that the family does not need the young person as a communication vehicle and the young person establishes a life of his or her own. Two extremes have often failed. Blaming the parents as a noxious influence and sending the young person away from his family typically fails. The young person collapses and comes back home. The opposite extreme of keeping the young person at home and attempting to bring about harmony between child and parents also fails. This is not a time of coming together but a time of disengagement. The act of therapy is to bring the young person back within the family as a way of discouraging him or her from a more independent life.

The key feature of such practice is the focus not only on what is happening in the client's situation but also on the wider system. This leads to the need to ask such questions as, what is the social worker's part in the maintenance of the problem? What are the expectations of the client system of social work? What are the agency expectations of the social worker and what are other agencies roles in relation to the situation? These questions help the worker and manager to develop a view of the problem which takes into account aspects of double description (Bateson 1980) by considering the problem from a number of vantage points. Having developed an hypothesis, social work intervention must focus on limited methods which relate specifically to the pattern of organisation of the system. As Haley (1980a) says: 'Understanding the systemic behaviour that created a malfunctioning hierarchy and planning ways to shift that hierarchy are the basic therapeutic tasks; other matters are peripheral.'

The requirement to be clear about the reason for intervention and to draw up an intervention strategy from the outset of social work involvement places a particular emphasis on the supervision of a social worker. In particular the supervisor must help the worker to have 'the ability and vision to understand the "rules" of the system and move beyond them' (Ross 1987), in other words the worker needs to be at a 'meta-level' from the client's situation in order to introduce new information into it. The social workers, once they get involved with a client and their family, group, or community, become accommodated to that system and react to the people in it, responding to the feelings, beliefs and actions of that system. Once in the system, if they are to remain a force for change within it they must be capable of maintaining a structured and ordered response to actions linked to the nature of their task. They cannot simply be buffeted by the actions of the members of the system. Seeing the 'wood for the trees' once involved is problematic, but the identification of pattern within the client-agency system is the key to being able to achieve manoeuvrability within the client system.

Much of family therapy addresses this problem in describing how the therapist rapidly becomes 'disqualified' or 'sucked into' a family once they accommodate to the family. Techniques such as using video, live supervision with a supervisor in the room when the therapist is working with a family, one-way screens and consultancy teams are part of family therapy practice and there have been some attempts to introduce them into mainstream social work practice. These may have some value but they remain only devices to try to help the worker and supervisor be clear about their objectives. There are difficulties if they are seen as ends in themselves, as necessities or prerequisites to a systems approach to social work. The important issue is that a social worker has to be clear about what they are trying to achieve and must constantly reassess the effects of their actions on their client and on the client's system. They must receive feedback about the effects of their actions. Without feedback the social worker receives no information about his/her impact and without that there can be no effective change. There is a continuous need to review what actions are being undertaken with clients, and the social worker must be substantially involved in a process of feedback and review.

Creative resolution based on minimum intervention

A further practice development of a systems approach is the idea of 'creative resolution' of problems. This phrase means that the social worker's action should be brief and direct to help maximise the resources of the client in her system. The social worker's interventions should be the minimum required to bring about an acceptable change and must be aimed at resolving rather than 'curing' the problem.

An example of this in the field of work with young offenders is the use of focused, offence-related material designed to make reparation for the crimes committed by young people. In one example of such a piece of work the client was a 16-year-old and was facing a court appearance on a charge of burglary and theft; he had pretended to be a door-to-door salesman, gained entry into an old lady's house and stolen money from her purse. This was the young man's seventh appearance in court, his first being for shoplifting when he was 12 years old, when he received a conditional discharge. After a further appearance for a similar offence he received more serious outcomes. His sixth court appearance was also for an offence of theft from elderly people.

This case demonstrates clearly the difference between a systems response, which defines the social work tasks in an ecological way, and other possible approaches. In this example the likely outcome, based on known responses of the juvenile justice system in that area gained from monitoring the system over time, was that this young man would receive a custodial sentence. The possible effects of that for the boy, though speculative, are fairly predictable. First, this boy, who was already a sophisticated and clever con man, would be involved for 24 hours every day with a highly delinquent peer group whilst in custody. This is often referred to as the 'contamination factor'. He would get to know a variety of other young men with whom he could form associations and attachments which would increase his opportunities and motivation to reoffend once he was released. At the same time, his links to his home, family and community would be weakened during the period of his sentence, perhaps even totally destroyed, which could have serious repercussions far beyond the sentence he was likely to receive. The 'ecology' of the boy's family system would be seriously and irrevocably affected by the 'event' of sentence.

It could be argued, from a different theoretical perspective, that the reasons for the boy's offending lay in disturbed family relationships, a deteriorated environment or negative peer influences and therefore removal from home to a non-custodial institution could be therapeutic but, in a systems perspective, it is essential to weigh up projected gains against the evidence produced by monitoring the outputs of the juvenile justice system. Reoffending rates for residential schools are no better (and in some studies rather worse) than those for custodial institutions, which are between 60 per cent and 80 per cent reconvicted within two years. The research evidence on delinquency (Hirschi 1971; Matza 1969) suggests that most young people do 'grow out' of offending. They 'put away childish things' once they integrate into adult society through employment, adult relationships, and obtaining the rights of adulthood. It is realistic to expect that this boy, despite his offending history, would integrate into adult society given time and encouragement, the support of his family and the help derived from mixing with other non-delinquent young people.

In a systems approach the role of the social worker is to encourage any positive influences to work for the boy, rather than against him. The task becomes one of trying to remove blocks that might stop this boy and his family handling the problems which threaten the ecology of their system. The 'traditional' social work response might have been to try to intervene in the system by finding a residential institution or to accept the inevitable custodial outcome and recommend nothing to the courts. This amounts to an acceptance that only punishment is appropriate, despite the research evidence that there is no deterrence in punishment. The social worker also has to deal with the demands of the system (the victim, public opinion, etc.) that this boy must be punished, or, at least, made to understand that his behaviour was unacceptable to society. 'Leaving the kids alone' was therefore not a possibility in this case, since this boy's crime was a serious one.

In this example a recommendation was put to the court that the boy should receive a supervision which had a number of components designed to 'resolve creatively' the offence. First, the boy would receive supervision which would try to help him and his family to deal with the problems that his behaviour was causing. A work placement was found for him and his parents were encouraged to help him get involved in appropriate leisure activities. Second, the boy would undertake eight two-hour sessions of reparation for his offences. The boy was assigned to a trained volunteer who picked up the laundry of housebound old people and took it to a laundry where the young man would wash and iron it for two hours every Saturday morning for eight weeks. The young man never saw where the old people lived nor was he involved in collecting or delivering the washing, since that could provide him with opportunities for getting into trouble with elderly people. Third, his supervising officer also took him to old people's homes, geriatric units and luncheon clubs to encourage him to learn about the nature of old age, particularly the effects of senile dementia, and help him try to understand the problems that old people might experience in the community. In this example, which is one of many similar attempts in the writers' experience to resolve offending behaviour creatively, the court accepted the recommendation, the boy undertook and completed the programme and some two years later was still in his own community and family without a further court appearance. This does not mean that all his problems were solved. He still had no job, got into fights with his friends and argued with his parents. Many would say his underlying problems still remained. However, within a systems framework, major ecological disasters had been avoided, his family system remained intact and he had not been further disadvantaged by the effects of incursive, unspecific social work intervention. Most important, he did not feel a sense of outrage against society. He did not feel the need to kick back at the agents of social control (police, adults, family, school and social workers) who punished him, because he understood the process in which he was involved and saw it as fair.

This example does show how social work practice, based on an ecology of intervention, means that the boy's context was understood and worked with, rather than an attempt being made to change his environment or destroy his connections with it. A normalising anti-pathological view of his behaviour was taken. His offences were serious and had to be dealt with, but were not considered indicative of deep emotional turmoil or psychological disturbance, inherently disturbed family relationship, or vast societal problems which individual social workers cannot change (such as unemployment or poverty). The intervention designed was brief and reconciled the court's desire to see that the boy received a sentence which was not overly lenient, the agency's need to offer help and yet maintain credibility with the court and the boy's need to stay out of custody or care yet be faced with the consequences of his actions. It attempted to resolve the immediate problem of his court appearance and had a 'fit' both with his situation and his behaviour – in other words he offended against old people and therefore he should pay back, in some way, to old people who were made vulnerable by his actions. Whilst the intervention did not allow him to live 'happily ever after', it maximised his opportunities to get a better deal from what society could offer him. Importantly, it did not create an embittered, alienated, disadvantaged youth out of a childish one. It did not make things worse by its attempted solutions.

The premise here is not that this intervention was the only one possible, or that there are no problems contained within this programme, but rather that it represented a creative attempt to resolve his problems which links with the evidence about how the juvenile justice system deals with young offenders, and the boy's real situation. Similarly, the concept of creative resolution can be applied to other kinds of social work if the focus of work is systemic, brief and problem focused.

Fit

Bateson's proposition that 'we might expect to find the same sort of laws at work, in the structure of a crystal as in the structure of society' (1980) suggests that the pattern and organisation of social systems has form and structure in the same way as organisms in the natural world. If this is accepted it is therefore important to try to relate social workers' interventions with individuals, families or groups to the internal pattern of their clients' systems.

The intervention made by the social worker should achieve a degree of 'fit' with the organisation of the family. For example, if a woman has used a cousin to care for her elderly dependent mother in other crisis situations, the most helpful intervention is likely to put resources into helping the cousin to continue to do this. That way it is likely that the social worker can 'go with' the system's natural ways of dealing with problems, rather than importing a new response. If social work decisions and interventions have a fit with the problem behaviour and with the organisational structure of the client's system then they work more effectively.

An example of this was a mother with two young children who were believed to be at risk when she had bouts of excessive drinking. They were helped to remain together by an arrangement whereby a neighbour was employed to look after the children on those occasions when the mother was incapable because of alcohol. This intervention had a 'fit' with the problem in several ways. First, it acknowledged that for the majority of the time this woman was perfectly able to parent her children responsibly. However, when she drank, she was not. Her drinking could not be condoned because of the risks to the children, yet unless she wished to stop she could not be helped to do so. This put more pressure on the family system. Choosing a local neighbour to care for the children for brief periods enabled the family system to remain intact with few risks to the children and also had a fit with the situation that existed for many other women in the community where, if they were incapacitated by illness or other factors, their friends, neighbours or family provided substitute care for their children. This woman was not able to enjoy this kind of help without welfare intervention to provide it.

This approach, like the reparation example quoted earlier, did not attempt to reform, cure or rearrange the client's system. It handled the legitimate area of social work concern, the risks to the children, without damaging the other aspects of the family system that were functioning appropriately. It also gave a clear message to the client that if she wanted to stop or start drinking that was her choice, but that she would not be allowed to put her children at risk.

This programme of social work intervention enabled the children to remain with their mother at home and in their own community. This contrasts with previous social work support over many years which involved removing the children into care whilst the mother, under this threat, agreed to attend Alcoholics Anonymous for several weeks, whereupon she got the children home. The mother's drinking would soon recommence and the children came in and out of care. Prior to this plan of involving a neighbour the social work department were contemplating removing the mother's parental rights.

The intervention described proved to be more effective than trying to make the woman totally abstemious or removing the children completely from home until their mother has 'proved' that she could stop drinking. Neither activity was very realistic, since no one gives up drinking because they are being threatened or punished and few parents ever prove themselves fit parents once their children are removed from them. The failure of social work to address issues of fit has a variety of consequences which are only too easily identified. In the area of fostering, for example, children are often placed with foster families who are diametrically different from their natural families in terms of class, wealth, culture, occupation, moral and religious beliefs and the internal family structures. Despite repeated references in the literature of fostering practice to the importance of 'matching', the reality in most social work agencies is for children of fragmented, poor, disordered families to be placed with close-knit, structured, middle-class, nuclear families and for those placements to break down with alarming frequency. The break down of fostering placements makes the child's situation worse, because they develop what might be termed 'secondary adjustment' problems in failing to cope with a new family. Rehabilitation at home, once child care interventions such as fostering have 'failed', becomes less likely since the social worker is usually unwilling to take any 'risky' decisions which might threaten either the child, his/her own professional status or that of the agency.

Haley describes the pressure that many social workers face in reconciling their social control function to protect clients and society from deviant behaviour and the need, in therapeutic terms, to be creative and take risks. In describing work aimed at returning home young people from a mental hospital he states (1980a):

> The therapeutic job is to bring about change and therefore new often unanticipated behaviour. The social control agent has quite the opposite goal. His task is to stabilise people for the community, thus he seeks to reduce unpredictability. He wants problem people to behave in acceptable ways, like others in the community, so that no-one is upset by them. It is not change and new behaviour that he seeks, but rather stability and no complaints from citizens. There is inevitably a conflict between a therapist whose job it is to encourage people to behave in new ways and a social controller who wants them to behave according to society's rules in predictable ways ... When the therapist says, 'Let us take this person out of custody, off medication and back into the community,' the social controller says, 'Let us not be irresponsible, let us proceed with caution.' Since there is a time and tide in the therapeutic enterprise and the therapist must take advantage of timing, caution is not always welcome. Often there is an optimum moment when parents will accept an offspring back home or when an opportunity arises, and the therapy can fail if action is not taken then.

Minimum interventions based on achieving some degree of fit with the client's system have more therapeutic potential in the long term. As Haley (1980a) says 'one can begin a small change and persistently amplifying it will change until the system adapting to it must reorganise'.

Achieving a fit in therapeutic intervention was a guiding principle behind the work of Milton Erickson. In his book *Uncommon Therapy: The Psychiatric Techniques of Milton H. Erickson* (1973), Haley describes how a man sought therapy because he could only urinate through a wooden tube. He had already had psychoanalysis and this had identified the 'cause' of his behaviour as rooted in a traumatic childhood experience whilst urinating, but this had not enabled the man to stop his embarrassing behaviour. Erickson asked the man first to change to a bamboo stick, which after all was a type of wood and was tubular. The man did as Erickson asked. Then Erickson asked him to make the length of the bamboo tube longer. This being successfully achieved he was asked to make it shorter. After a number of sessions the man was able to urinate through a bamboo tube which was only a few inches long. Erickson suggested that he then consider how his penis actually was a tube and how the fingers of his hand could form a kind of tube through which he could urinate. Thus the man 'resolved' his problem and developed a 'normal' if rather self-conscious way of performing his bodily functions. Erickson did not demand a major change in the man's behaviour. He did not introduce major new elements into the system such as drugs, intrapsychic explanations for his behaviour or removal from his environment into hospital. He concentrated on creating a small change in the pattern of the man's behaviour and thus gave the man the ability to bring the problem under some voluntary control. He was able to normalise the behaviour, suggesting that all men urinate through a 'tube' of sorts, rather than trying to challenge directly the man's view that it was abnormal. Bateson says of Erickson 'Milton worked in the weave of the total complex' (1973) and it is this and Bradford Keeney's concept of family therapy when 'head and heart become part of the cybernetic system capable of ecological self-correction' (1983) which is suggested for ecological practice in social work.

As Haley points out, Erickson not only communicated with patients in metaphors, but also 'worked within the metaphor to bring about a change'(1973). Social workers have to find a fit between their responses and intervention with their clients, and the difficulties in this cannot be minimised since they often have to deal with very varied groups of individuals in the full range of human situations. They require the capacity to engage with a variety of individuals and also to link their work to the many problem situations they encounter. In systems terms, the problem behaviours that bring people to social workers are, themselves, attempts by the client to solve systems dilemmas and, as such, have to be worked with rather than removed.

Reframing

Linked to the concept of fit is the notion of reframing, already described in Chapter 3.

Examples of reframing occur frequently in everyday life – a pint glass of beer can be 'half full' or 'half empty', but the descriptions have a different meaning for the listener. The 'facts' are not changed by reframing, but the context of them or the meaning ascribed to them creates a new set of beliefs or perceptions about them. Once people see things differently, they behave differently in relation to that information – thus allowing for 'news of difference' which makes a difference. These acts of reframing are central to developing a fit with the client's viewpoints and value system and helping them change that behaviour.

It is also possible to reframe using 'meaning' reframes. An example in the writers' experience of reframing by changing the meaning occurred when a woman was complaining that when her husband got home from work he sat down in the armchair and fell asleep for several hours. She was congratulated that he felt he needed to rest to prepare himself to enjoy fully the stimulation of her company and presence during the night. Examples of context and meaning reframes are not verbal tricks on the part of therapists. They are attempts to widen the client's understanding of their world. As Minuchin says, 'people are continuously moulded by their contexts and their characteristics elicited by contexts' (1974). Minuchin and Fishman (1981) describe how:

> in Wonderland, Alice suddenly grew to a gigantic size. Her experience was that she got bigger while the room got smaller. If Alice had grown in a room that was also growing at the same rate, she might have experienced everything staying the same. Only if Alice and the room change separately does her experience change. It is simplistic, but not inaccurate, to say that intrapsychic therapy concentrated on changing Alice. A structural family therapist concentrates on changing Alice within her room.

Minuchin describes the type of treatments received by a woman who first experienced traditional psychiatry and then received treatment from a 'context-related therapist' who saw the woman's behaviour as indicative of an ecological crisis. The case study is worthy of a full description here because the therapist is working in an ecological way.

Minuchin describes an Italian widow in her late 60s who had lived in the same apartment for 25 years. She was robbed one day. She decided to leave her apartment and called a furniture removal firm. The people came to move her but she said they tried to control where she went. They moved her belongings, they misplaced and lost her precious possessions. They left cryptograms on her furniture and secretly signalled to each other. She went to a psychiatrist, who gave her tranquillisers, but her experience did not change. He purposely left bottles on the table for her which she thought were dangerous. He recommended inpatient treatment and then hospitalisation, but she refused. Minuchin contrasts this with 'another therapist, whose interventions were based on an ecological understanding of the old and lonely'. He explained that she was like a crustacean that had 'lost its shell' and she was vulnerable – her problems would disappear when she 'grew a new shell'. She was to unpack her belongings and make it like her old apartment. She was to create a routine – getting up at a certain time, shopping on the same day, and so on. She was not to make new friends, but to visit her old ones. In order to spare her family, she was not to describe any of her experiences and if anyone were to ask, she was to explain that her problems 'were merely the problems of illogical, fearful, old people'. This was to block what Minuchin described as 'the paranoid community that had developed around her' and was amplifying her reactions to her new environment (negative feedback). As her experience and understanding of her circumstances changed, so her symptoms, which were functional responses to the experiences of her life, disappeared.

As well as using reframing directly with a client or their system it can also be used with the wider systems that pathologise clients' behaviour. For example a 12-year-old boy was appearing before a children's panel for a second time for not attending school. When he tried to go to school, he developed headaches, sweated profusely and became physically sick. His mother had attempted to take him to school but was fearful of making him ill and was unwilling to continue. He had seen a psychologist who felt he was 'too closely bonded' to his mother and needed residential schooling and recommended that the children's panel make an order with which to commit the child to a residential school. The boy and his mother were terrified this might occur and refused to see anyone to talk about the situation. The social worker hypothesised that this behaviour would be seen as uncooperative by the boy and his mother towards the panel, and would be seen as indicative that 'compulsory measures of care' were necessary to help the boy. She reframed their behaviour in her report and presentation to the panel as indicative of the very important close relationship between the boy and his mother that sustained them even in the most difficult times. The boy genuinely needed help for school phobia, but in order for this to be gradually and carefully given, so that he could slowly be desensitised about school, there must be no external pressures on the boy, such as threats of removal from home – which would make him and his mother so anxious that they would not be able to undertake the treatment successfully. The role of the children's panel was reframed by the social worker as their having an opportunity to help the boy realise that he would get better and return to school, but that it could take time and would require him to keep on trying.

The panel should not make any statutory order since the boy had to want to be helped, without threats of compulsion. They agreed on the recommendation and he has slowly and successfully been reintroduced to an ordinary school.

In this example the reframing was more important in the wider system than for the child himself. Sometimes the reframing is directly with the client's system. A child's 'hyperactivity' might be described as 'boisterous', or a series of rows might be described as 'how this family show how much they care about each other'. In any reframe, the description must find a fit with the values and beliefs of the system it describes; only thus can it be effective in widening the beliefs and behaviour of the client system. Milton Erickson was a great exponent of such an approach to changing his client's behaviour. Like the judo master, he used his patient's force by going with it, rather than against it (Erickson, Rossi and Rossi 1976): 'You suggest that they withhold – and they do. But they withhold and they tell responsively. And as long as they are going to withhold, you ought to encourage them to withhold.' Erickson believed that the client's value system was the road into their communication. When introduced to a man on a psychiatric ward who believed he was Jesus Christ, he said 'I believe you are very familiar with carpentry' and gave him some useful joinery to do.

Reframing is an effective method of expanding the context of behaviours and beliefs in the client's and the wider systems that define their difficulties and problems and is an essential part of an ecology of practice.

Circularity in social work practice

A critical problem in applying systems ideas in social work is the linear epistemology which is evidenced in most of its theory and practice. It is an interesting, but sad, fact that linear thinking frequently leads to vicious spirals (like 'more of the same' loops mentioned earlier, self-fulfilling prophecies and the like). Linear interpretations of clients' behaviour abound in social work from the crude explanations of 'lack of maternal bonding' between a mother and her baby 'creating' tension and unhappiness in their subsequent lives, to social histories of young people containing information about whether they were breast-fed and reached their 'milestones' at the appropriate time. More insidiously erroneous notions of linear causation exist such as poverty and unemployment in families 'causing' family breakdown, bad behaviour in children, non-attendance at school and the like. As has been emphasised, social workers acting on linear notions commit an epistemological error that can have significant effects on the lives of children and families.

Rejecting the concept of linear causation and accepting that there are no absolute 'truths' when one asks why people behave in certain ways is of fundamental significance for social workers. Acting as if human behaviour is caused by the action of one person's behaviour on another, or a set of circumstances in someone's life creating certain types of responses, leads to what Bateson terms 'higher orders of pathology' (1980). Notions that we can programme people to behave differently or give them a different set of experiences which will 'cause' them to change their behaviour are part of that false and bad epistemology that ultimately harms through attempts to help. These fallacious notions have had their impact on most forms of social work and they are professional Aunt Sallys which have proved remarkably unwilling to lie down (Ross 1984).

For example, in *Measure of Diversion* (Adams *et al.* 1981), when describing a groupwork programme for young people in trouble, Ward suggested that:

> through controlled learning experiences and achievements, delinquent norms and anti-authoritarian values could be replaced by more socially acceptable behaviour and better relationships with adults, particularly those in authority. Discipline and decision-making were to be based as far as possible on democratic therapeutic community principles ... the workers intended to develop horizontal relationships with children.

Apart from the mystification of the language in Ward's description of his group, the notion that children's relationships with adults in one situation would generalise into other situations and cause significant changes in their behaviour outside of the group is nonsense. It is based on the linear notion that good experiences in one context lead to changes in behaviour in another – a notion with no supporting research evidence and refuted by Bateson's learning experiments described earlier. Social workers must have this kind of notion continually challenged in their practice so that linear fallacies, which frequently lead to punitive, harsh, unrealistic and unrealisable outcomes for clients, are not pursued.

Social work agendas with clients can be specific, relevant and attainable. Inevitably, our linear language will create problems and mean that descriptions of human behaviour are partial and inadequate, but understanding this is a key to an ecology of practice. Weakland's comments on the flaws in Bateson's research project, of which he was a part, sum up the limited position which social work arrives at in its epistemological questions (1981):

> The basic problem our work faced goes even beyond the obstinate fact that our subject, as well as our tool for handling it, involves words. The root of the matter is that, for all its variety and flexibility, language is only part of communication and behaviour. The concrete whole cannot be conceptualised within the specialist part – sad as this realisation must be to all of us who, as scientists and scholars, specialise in putting matters into words. One can, at most, depict certain slices of the larger reality in words well enough to be helpful, for certain limited purposes – so long as one keeps realising the account is only partial.

Importantly, there is strong evidence (Thomas and Millichamp 1985; Bilson 1986) to suggest that the contents of social inquiry reports significantly increased the likelihood of harsher outcomes such as residential care and custody for young people (Thomas and Millichamp 1985):

> Many of those reports which recommended custody seemed to be replete with details of non-criminal behaviour which was judged by adults (parents, teachers, social workers) to be unacceptable ... There needs to be a fundamental reappraisal of how social enquiry reports are prepared in terms of format and content. So many of the reports we view are just time-chronicled 'bad news-sheets' presented in such a way as almost to create a feeling of hopelessness in the minds of the courts which blocks magistrates' sentencing and leads to custody.

Because reports and the writings of social workers are the vehicle through which the ideologies of social workers are expressed, an important strategy in systems practice is to direct effort towards the nature of reports. This is necessary in reports for courts and hearings where their language and contents can lead to removal from home. Changing reports involves embarking on extensive in-service training programmes for social workers as well as checking, and analysing reports and their outcomes for the client by social work managers within agencies.

In the writers' experience of undertaking this in three local authorities with different legal systems, the results of such a strategy became very quickly evident. Gratuitously irrelevant, negative information which suggests causation has to be challenged and replaced by descriptions of the client's situation which have a direct bearing on the problem. In the case of children, for example, it is possible to achieve the removal of implied direct causal links between a multitude of unrelated issues, such as the behavioural characteristics of the subject's parents (drinking, uncooperative response to social workers, etc.), some of which are about areas of the client's experience over which he/she will have no control whatsoever. Most of the latter kind of information can be left out of reports without any loss of accuracy for the judicial process since much is unsubstantiated gossip and speculation about the client's life.

The following brief extracts from reports submitted to children's panels in an agency before a report-writing strategy and after it had been implemented, graphically demonstrate the differences. Simon (aged 14) was referred to a children's hearing for minor offences of theft.

> Mrs S and Simon have remained cooperative. Mr S has not attended any meetings, apparently taking the view that as Simon is the person who is on supervision, only he should be seen. Relationships within the family remain largely the same, although Simon has stated that he feels his relationship with his father has deteriorated. Simon feels his father picks on him and is generally unfair, though I am uncertain how true this is. Mrs S remains protective towards Simon and, at times, they appear to be more like husband and wife than mother and son. Recently Mrs S has stated that she has reduced her alcohol intake, and Simon appears to have been a main force in bringing about this change, as he has taken on the role of regulating Mrs S's drinking. Mr S continues to view his wife's drinking as a non-problem. Simon's period of supervision has not resulted in any change. While I have to acknowledge:
>
> a. that the period of supervision we are considering has been brief;
>
> b. that I may well have had a part to play in this lack of change;
>
> I have, from the outset, been doubtful about the family's capacity to change and whether Simon would be able to achieve some distance from his mother, and in my opinion my original doubts have been confirmed.
>
> Simon's attitude towards his involvement in the offence concerns me as he was dismissive and almost jovial. However, Simon's involvement in the offences does not appear to be taken seriously by the family. They appear to have reached a stage where they are almost accepting his behaviour. Simon has stated that he would like to leave the family home due to his poor relationships with his family. His mother would rather this did not occur, however, she accepts that this may be inevitable. I do not know Mr S's views on this matter …

> Regretfully, Simon still appears to be a rather vulnerable boy and may well be involved in further offences. After carefully considering his situation, in my opinion, Simon would have the greatest hope of changing if he had a period of residential supervision. Such a move cannot guarantee that he would not be involved in further offences. However, I believe that such a placement would hopefully:
>
> a. offer Simon a clearer structure and boundaries;
>
> b. offer distance from his mother, although such a move would not automatically achieve emotional distance.
>
> I therefore respectfully recommend that he be placed on supervision with a condition of residence. I have contacted Westdale List D school and asked them if they would consider offering Simon a place.

The social background report written before the report-writing strategy resulted in a care order with a condition to go to a residential school. Within six months the boy was in secure accommodation and from there he went to custody at 16 years of age. The negative insinuation of causal connections between unmotivated parents and the boy's offending led to negative consequences for the boy's ecology. The report contrasts with the following report written after the strategy. Martin was 14 and appeared before the children's hearing for non-attendance at school:

> Martin clearly continues to have very real distress related to attendance at school. He is not a boy who simply 'refuses' to attend, more someone who finds he cannot go despite a very real desire to be a normal schoolboy. Despite his anxiety that he may end up being placed away from home because of his appearance at the Children's Hearing, he has made a real effort to work with Child Guidance and this has been a major step both for him and his family. He appears to become extremely anxious when he is away from home and we will be continuing to try to help Martin and his mother deal gradually with the reintegration into normal school and leisure activities as would be appropriate to boys of his age.
>
> In reality, given Martin's degree of difficulty, it is likely that he will continue to have anxieties about school attendance for a considerable length of time, however, he is receiving education at the Child Guidance Unit and the family are fully complying with all the agencies involved – my department, education, the hospital and Child Guidance.

> In considering a suitable disposal for the Hearing, I do not feel a residential placement would be in Martin's best interests and I think he would find the separation from home impossible to cope with and there is clear evidence that even a threat of such a possibility is causing him real distress. While a Supervision Order would formalise this Department's contact with the family, it would have absolutely no bearing on improving Martin's attendance at school and I feel it may increase his suspicion of social workers. This family cooperate well on a voluntary basis with all agencies trying to help and Martin would do also, so long as this does not involve any form of compulsion.
>
> The family are working well with all the various agencies and arrangements for Martin to receive the help he needs are currently under way and there are signs of progress in his work with Child Guidance.
>
> I would recommend that the Panel discharge the referral at this time, given that he is getting the help that he and his family need. He is caused suffering by what he sees as the threat of removal from home which the attendance at the Children's Hearing represents to him and he can only be helped through his problem by patient encouragement, not by pressure through statutory involvement. My Department will continue to work with Martin and his family on a voluntary basis until he is returned to full time education.

In this case the children's panel discharged the referral with no compulsory measures being taken, despite having asked the social worker at the previous hearing to seek a residential placement and the recommendation of a consultant psychiatrist that he be taken into care. The report is specific, realistic and clear in its recommendation and it offers no notions of causality or blame. It represents an attempt to deal with the boy within his ecology.

Notions of circularity are crucial to an ecology of social work practice. The eradication of fallacious linear notions can be aided by a concentration on the written word – particularly social enquiry reports, case histories, letters and case notes. What is said defines what is thought and what is acted upon. Thus a vital part of an ecology of practice is to have an impact on the way social workers write about and understand their clients and thus the way they define their tasks.

Conclusion

The shift from the theories of systemic thought to the pragmatics of action by social workers with clients is extraordinarily difficult. Bateson's distaste for pragmatics and his professional rebuttals of men like Carl Rogers, Jay Haley and, to some extent, even Milton Erickson himself, make fascinating reading even many years after they occurred. They represent the tension between systems ideas about the organisations of families at one level of logical typing and the actions of people and their helpers at another. Frequently the two are confused and distortions and myths such as that of 'power' in relationships, which disturbed Bateson so much, are thus created. Families, for example, are seen as using 'homeostatic mechanisms' to avoid changing as if these are identifiable 'things', actions or behaviours which can be encountered as one meets with families in one's work. In his article 'The place of family therapy in the homeostasis of larger systems' (1982), Coppersmith says:

> Family Therapy may contribute to problems rather than ameliorate them by applying interventions at the wrong level of the system. Working within the boundaries of the family, when the correct level for intervention is either that of the interface of the family in larger systems, or within the larger systems, may place the Family Therapist in the paradoxical position of supporting stress by the very actions intended to relieve stress.

This is a critical issue for social workers trying to work ecologically and is why this book does not make a case for the establishment of family therapy clinics or for the broad establishment of family therapy in agencies. Social workers must not lose sight of their responsibility to intervene at the level in the client system at which they 'hypothesise that change can be encouraged'. If they see themselves as family therapists, their inevitable focus will be on the behaviour of the family members, regardless of whether that is where the greatest threat to the family lies. As Coppersmith says:

> Representatives of larger systems may blame the parents for a problem in the child, or blame the child and sympathise with the parents or may blame the entire family, under the rubric of being 'unmotivated' or in some other way defective. With the increased popularity of family therapy, such larger systems have began to make referrals to family therapy, in order to 'fix' the family in much the same way that identified patients have been sent by their families to treatment to be 'fixed'. Such a shift from individual blame to family blame is, in fact, no change at all.

The important thrust of intermediate treatment practice in the late 1970s and 1980s, particularly as defined by Thorpe *et al.* (1980), was to direct effective social work with juvenile offenders towards 'systems management' techniques which had the principal aim of keeping the young person out of institutional care or custody. Thorpe, like Bateson, refutes decontextualised methods and techniques (1980):

> If the past decades have shown anything, it is that 'good ideas' and new techniques are simply not enough. It would be easy to write a handbook of method, an inchoate list of activities, games and therapeutic stratagems, but it would change nothing. Techniques are meaningless if practiced on the wrong people, in the wrong setting and for the wrong reasons ... we are trying to bring about a fall from grace. It is time to bite the apple and realise that there is more to social work with delinquents, or anyone else than the last activity, fad or the most recently imported therapeutic cult.

He goes on to talk about 'the necessary rebuilding of conceptual foundations' which direct social workers back to the epistemological issues of what social work is about.

Social workers are key definers in what happens to clients. The way they 'frame' reports, describe the client to each other and to other powerful parts of the system (such as psychiatrists, police, children's hearings, courts, doctors etc.) and exercise statutory controls in their lives give them opportunities to destroy or preserve the ecology of the client's system. The principles described in this chapter of creating order, creative resolution, fit, reframing and circularity represent guidelines for social workers to handle consciously epistemological concerns within a framework of systems understanding. Their intervention may be at the interface between the family and larger systems, it may be with an individual or it may be within their own agency system to reframe a client's actions, but what they do has an effect which must be recognised and understood.

One of Bateson's key phrases was 'you cannot not have an epistemology'. The contention of this chapter is that there are, at the heart of all social work activities, notions about how systems change, develop and maintain themselves. It is possible to practise social work in a way which preserves, values and protects the ecology of families and which minimises the levels and effects of state intervention in client's lives. This ecology of practice throws social workers and their managers into epistemological questions about what they are doing. This is not an easy way to work and it can have no easy appeal. Brockman's introduction to his book *About Bateson* sums up the issues perfectly in a brief paragraph (1977):

> But this is where Bateson gets difficult. Just what is this 'new scientific territory'? Most people look for the next place, the next piece of knowledge. Instead, Bateson presents an epistemology so radical that as one climbs from step to step, the ground supporting the ladder abruptly vanishes. Not easy, this cybernetic explanation of Gregory Bateson. Not comfortable. Not supportive. Not loving.

However difficult and challenging it may be, we suggest that social work can accommodate systems ideas and that these ideas provide a better way of both explaining and guiding practice. Systems concepts are better fitted to handle the complexity of human organisations, not by generating rules for practice, but by providing principles which are more effective in guiding practice than the alternatives which the profession has maintained.

Summary

Systems practice means considering clients in relation to their 'lifespace' or 'ecology'. Social work with clients has to be undertaken in the context of the client's real life situation, not some idealised or Utopian perception of what the client needs or wants. The interconnectedness of their situation, behaviour and belief system with that of other members of their social system must be allowed for since any intervention in that social system by the social worker will have effects throughout it.

The 'pattern' of the interaction within the client-agency system is the key determinant of the outcome of social work actions and targets must be established and maintained in the management of the case. The practice of the social worker with client(s) and the management of the case will:

1. create order in the client–worker system through a clear definition of roles and tasks
2. aim to resolve problems creatively where possible, through minimum intervention
3. ensure that any social work interventions have a 'fit' with the beliefs, behaviour and lifestyle of the client and his social system
4. reframe attitudes and beliefs of the client, or within the client's social system, which block effective resolution of problems, in order to change their meaning or context

5. remove cause and effect analysis of a linear nature of the client's problem, particularly from reports, letters and case summaries. Circular definitions of problems should be developed.

CHAPTER 5

Case Studies in Practice

Bringing about Changes for Families and Individuals using Systems Approaches

> If 'a systems approach' is to become more than an easily accepted, but somewhat irritating concept, there is a need for expressions of it which eliminate any difference between what it is and how we may use it. The need is for systems based methodologies which describe a systems approach as a way of analysing and hence trying to solve real world problems.
>
> P.B. Checkland, *Towards a Systems based Methodology for Real World Problem-Solving (1981)*

A systems approach to social work practice contains the key elements described and summarised in the last chapter. These will be illustrated in this chapter by two case studies which show a systems analysis of very different situations dealt with by a social work agency. It shows, too, the actions of the workers involved based on that systems analysis. In these examples, the identified clients will be considered in relation to their ecology or life-space. The interconnectedness of their situation with the behaviour and beliefs of others will be examined. The pattern of their interaction with the agency, and vice versa, will be described and a working hypothesis will be suggested as a realistic focus for the work.

The case studies here are not presented as the only way of dealing with the difficulties experienced by the clients they describe – they are not flawless models of good practice acting as beacons of light for other social workers to follow. Nor are they methods and approaches of a 'cookbook' variety whereby doing the same thing in similar cases will produce similar outcomes. We are suggesting rather that they illustrate systems principles in the real world and that they show how systems ideas can help workers develop approaches in practice which acknowledge the potential to harm clients through intervention, as well as to help them. They are described in order to demonstrate that systems approaches to practice help social workers to decide on realistic and achievable ways to work with clients which take into account the uniqueness of their situation, but also predict some potential areas of difficulty. They may look very similar to other theoretical frameworks and methods in social work and we do not claim that what has been done in them in terms of practice is either highly imaginative or unique. What is most important in these examples is the way of looking at and conceptualising the social work problems being addressed which is, as we maintain throughout this book, the fundamental issue in a systems approach to social work management and practice.

The first example is of Mr M. He was 64 years old. The agency received three separate referrals about him in one day, one from his local councillor, one from the police and one from the fire brigade, all concerned with the public health risk this man was causing to himself and to the local community. Piecing together the information on him available at that time, the problem appeared thus. He was living alone following his wife's death eight years previously. He liked a drink (the police believed he was an alcoholic), he did not clean his house at all and he cooked by burning rubbish in a bucket in the centre of his living-room. He lived in his own flat in a respectable tenement of privately owned dwellings. His neighbours were terrified that they were going to be burnt alive by fires which would start in his flat, unnoticed by him. He had returned home recently, having been hospitalised following a fire caused by such an accident.

In this example, the social work agency worked with him in an unplanned way for two years before a reappraisal and adoption of a systems approach to his difficulties was undertaken. It is important to look at the two-year history of agency involvement to determine the pattern of interaction which developed between the social workers and the client, a pattern which needs to be unpicked if a systems approach is to be undertaken. Whatever the history of agency involvement with a client, it is crucial to make some working hypothesis or definition of the interaction between the agency and the client as was shown in the previous chapter. The first worker to deal with Mr M attempted to define his task at the point of referral and this is obviously important so as to avoid the suck-in effect of social systems, to be clear about the social work focus and to introduce order into the social worker's approach to the client. However, his analysis does little to keep the social work agenda clear, as will be shown. He says in the case notes:

> I feel the house needs to be thoroughly cleaned but gradually, with the person/persons gaining Mr M's confidence as they proceed and encouraging him to help and take an interest. He is wary of people at first as he has led a rather isolated life and is not happy if too many people visit.

As far as this assessment goes, it is a reasonable analysis of the issues for the work though, interestingly, he does not make reference to what Mr M says he wants or needs, or anything about the client's social system; nor does it attempt to assess the level of risk. This was particularly important in this case as a major reason for referral was the fear of the neighbours who were terrified of being burnt to death in a fire. His opening case notes do not look, either, at any of the resources which the client is already using in trying to deal with the issues for himself. The worker also notes in the case file that on the first occasion he saw Mr M he threatened the client with the National Assistance Act 1947 (giving the local authority powers to compulsorily remove people from their homes if they put other people's lives at risk by their lifestyle). He also offered him a bed in an old people's home and a home help. It is interesting how his assessment talks of gaining Mr M's confidence though, in reality, the solutions offered were anything but gradual in the threat that they would pose to his current lifestyle, were he to accept them. Mr M refused all such offers and did not acknowledge any difficulties to the worker. The worker purchased a cooker for him so that he could stop cooking over a bucket (ironically, the cooker was plugged into a faulty electric socket which proved a further fire risk some weeks later!) and he gave him some groceries which he accepted. The worker visited at three-weekly intervals from that point on though, very often, Mr M was out when he called. Three months later the worker stated:

> The house was again untidy around the bed and chair, i.e. milk cartons, cigarette ends everywhere. I cleaned the room with Mr M's assistance and agreed to supply a few refuse sacks. Mr M, although enjoying a chat, did not feel the need for social work involvement. He did not foresee his lifestyle changing and was content with the way it was. I offered him one day a week in an old people's home where he could have a bath and wash his dirty clothes. Mr M refused this offer without consideration.

The worker at this point had clear expectations about how the man should live which the client did not share, though he continued with his initial plan to build up the man's confidence by working alongside him to clean the flat on his visits. The risk to others from fire does not appear in the notes at all but seems to have become blurred with the issues of cleanliness and hygiene addressed by the worker in trying to provide 'solutions' or 'ready remedies' such as an old people's home or a home help. The client had still not been involved in defining the problems for which he wanted help. Despite some evidence that he was making the gradual relationship with Mr M that the worker claimed could help him to help and take an interest, the notes indicate that the worker was getting frustrated by the lack of changes in this man's lifestyle and he reflects in the case notes that there was

> little point to social work involvement at this time. I tried in vain to negotiate further work with Mr M but he was non-committal and again expressed his wish that no home help should be involved.

Then, during one of his visits six months later, the worker notes that:

> suddenly during the conversation, he told me he believed his father had committed suicide. His father had become rather depressed after his wife's death and smothered himself with a pillow. I took from his comments that he was giving me an indication of how he might wish to terminate his life.

The worker does not seem to have shared this expectation with the client but he continued to visit him at intervals of three weeks and this does not seem to have changed his assessment or work focus in any way. It is unclear why he believed it worthy of note. He continued to offer a place in an old people's home, home-help services and day-care services which Mr M always refused, and he sometimes took him money or groceries which Mr M always accepted. Nearly 18 months after the original referral the worker refused him money for groceries when Mr M asked for it and notes:

> He threatened to kill himself and I told him I would see him in a fortnight. He replied by saying that he would probably be dead by then.

At this point a new social worker took over Mr M's case and she comments that she agrees with the previous worker's views of Mr M's situation, though there is no definition of what she considered these to be. She talks to Mr M about his past and suggests that home-help services should be offered him, which he continues to refuse. Quite often when she calls he is out. In her case notes she defines her role: 'because no one else visits, my role is a monitoring one as to his safety and well being.' It is only in the case notes two years after opening the case that anyone mentions the man's environment or social system. When the worker visited on that occasion, Mr M was again out. She notes:

> the smell going up the tenement stairs was extremely bad, the odour of urine coming from his flat was overpowering. Out of concern as to his safety, she asked a neighbour if she had seen him recently. Her case notes say the neighbour replied: 'he is still going about though I have not seen him today.'

The neighbours were again asked a month later how he was when the worker called and found him out. They said, on that occasion, that he seemed all right but their main concern was still his habit of 'burning stuff in the house'.

A student social worker then took over the case. She again threatened him with the National Assistance Act 1947 and asked him to accept a home help or 'a holiday' in a home. The neighbours were noted as saying to her that he 'may still be burning rubbish in the house as they had smelt smoke on one occasion a few days ago'. The case was then closed when the student's placement finished because she said 'she did not see the need for any further social work involvement'.

The case was reopened two months later when Mr M was admitted to hospital following a further fire in his flat. The flat was now considered a very serious health hazard with filth, rubbish and human excrement littering the living areas. Similarly, large areas of the flat were burnt and virtually derelict. Mr M was shocked but otherwise unhurt by the fire. At this point, a reappraisal of the involvement of the agency had to be undertaken with a clear redefinition of approach.

It could be seen that the pattern of social work involvement followed a 'more of the same' loop where the workers had tried to get him to accept a standard package of resources which he felt were unnecessary. The more they pushed the less he did for himself and the more he withdrew and became dependent on the gifts of food. The neighbours got increasingly anxious as they saw the efforts of social workers being frustrated by Mr M, who was frequently out when they called. The neighbours felt that the authorities were not taking their fear of fire seriously. The workers had been genuinely concerned about this man's feelings of loneliness and isolation and had got him to talk about his previous life which may indeed have increased his sense of loss in his current situation. When he hinted that he might feel like taking his own life, the worker did not visit him for a further three weeks and very soon after that, transferred the case. The problem for which he was originally referred, that is, the fire and health risk, was only marginally alluded to as the workers began to content themselves with a 'monitoring role', despite the evidence in the late part of the case notes that his whereabouts were already being monitored very closely by the neighbours who knew when they had seen him and when he had last burnt rubbish in the flat. These neighbours were not seen as part of the context of this man's situation and there is no assessment of the possible help that they were being in containing the risks to this man in his own home. Reading the case notes, one might almost be forgiven for assuming that the social worker and Mr M were alone on a desert island where nothing else contributed to their interaction but their own discussions. Money and groceries were given sporadically to Mr M when the worker considered it appropriate although the abiding theme in the case notes is the frustration of the worker that Mr M would not accept other 'help' such as a home help, a place in an old people's home or day care. This frustration can be an important determinant of social work help – as Hoffman (1996) says, 'Hell hath no fury like a helping agent scorned'. It was important that a realistic redefinition of the social work task was made in order to avoid punitive responses to this man. An assessment of his needs could not take place without these issues being addressed by the social work agency.

The first priority, therefore, for a systems approach was to see this man in his social context. Second, a definition of his problem had to be arrived at which he and everyone else could understand. Third, resources must be identified which could deal with the identified problem. Fourth, the pattern of social work involvement, which was to attempt by bullying, bribery and persuasion to make him do things he did not want to do, must now change.

In order to define the degree of risk to himself and others that this man constituted a case conference was called. His GP, his local councillor and other important figures in the social network were asked to attend and were required specifically to comment on what resources might be brought in to help lessen the risk to him in his own home. They were also asked to describe what attempts had been made to help this man in the past since, in a systems perspective, attempted solutions often maintain existing problems. At this case conference, and in subsequent discussions with the workers involved, there was a definition of the problem which had to be focused on risk caused by his habit of burning paper in the middle of the room and his lack of hygiene. Within these discussions, attention was paid to how those concerns could be discussed with Mr M in a way that would lead him to see the problem as something which he needed to deal with.

It was agreed that resources would only be used in this case to address the issues of his personal hygiene and his setting fires. No money or services would be offered to Mr M which were not specifically related to attempts to resolve these problems.

A social work assistant visited him in hospital and started to see him twice a week when he was discharged in order to carry out practical tasks which Mr M acknowledged he found difficult, such as shopping, cleaning and budgeting. He was temporarily housed in homeless persons' accommodation and his social worker then looked with him, and with his neighbours, at the state of his flat and the fire risks and health hazards that it had become. Smoke detectors were fitted, not only to his flat, but to the adjoining staircase so that the neighbours would be immediately alerted if he started burning any material. Thus, their existing monitoring function was acknowledged and they were seen as being the most able people in his social system to undertake that task effectively. The fire brigade were asked for specialist advice on how best to protect Mr M and the other residents of the flats, and the neighbours began to feel that, for the first time, the social work department was not ignoring their concerns and taking sides with Mr M against them. The social worker took Mr M back to his flat and walked around it with him pointing out to him the reason why the flat was considered a health hazard in very blunt language. Mr M reluctantly acknowledged its terrible state and, following this visit, agreed to allow the environmental health department to fumigate his flat and volunteers to redecorate it. He went with the social work assistant to see his GP to examine whether his feelings of loneliness were associated with any kind of treatable depression. The GP pronounced him 'extremely healthy mentally and physically for his age', but warned him to take a better diet in order to keep well. This was a particularly important piece of information for the social worker who had felt, up to that point, that Mr M might be behaving as he had because of a 'clinical depression' or some unresolved grief from his wife's death. This kind of belief, based on a pathologising of behaviour, can easily distract the worker from a focus of work which had been agreed and could have led the worker back into discussions with this man about his past life rather than his current difficulties. There was some evidence that such discussions compounded Mr M's feelings of inadequacy and loss and it was important that social work efforts remained focused solely on the issues of risk to Mr M in the community.

Similarly, the issues of removal from home were categorically rejected since Mr M neither wanted nor needed to leave his own home. It was stated to him and to all those involved with him that no attempts would be made by the social work department to persuade him to give up his flat against his wishes. All the social work efforts from now on would be put into helping him with the problems he would experience when he returned to the flat.

There were clearly no Utopian solutions for Mr M's difficulties. He returned home and allowed the social work assistant and the social worker to help him to keep the flat reasonably clean and ensure that he did not light fires in it. The neighbours remained concerned about him and they are still the most important resource in maintaining his safety in the community. His lifestyle changed only marginally but there were some small signs that he was prepared to accept regular practical help. A systems approach in dealing with his situation allowed for the 'pattern' of social work involvement with him to be reshaped and more realistically designed in accordance with his social situation.

The second case study involved a boy called Stewart and his family. Social work involvement with him began when he was 14 years old and his mother contacted the social work department because he was 'out of her control'. His mother said to the social worker: 'These problems cannot be solved within the family without outside help.'

Stewart was said to be losing his temper and acting aggressively towards his mother. She believed it was because he resented her cohabitee, who had been with her since Stewart was aged one, but she felt Stewart had 'never accepted her separation from her husband and still wished they could be reunited'. From a systems point of view the family's beliefs about what led to the problems are important, and also their attempted solutions to the problem are to be considered. In this situation, the way they dealt with the conflicts were that Stewart's mother appealed for outside help to the police, the reporter to the children's panel, the school, child guidance and finally to the social work department. She clearly believed that solutions to her son's difficulties would come from outside the family and, as the helping agencies moved in and tried to convince the family that they had to change in their handling of Stewart, the situation worsened. Shortly after the original referral, Stewart was removed from home following a family row which ended with his mother calling the police.

The working systems hypothesis in this case, following removal, was that Stewart's behaviour was part of a normal adolescent conflict with his mother and stepfather. However, when Stewart lost his temper with his mum, she appealed to her cohabitee to control him which Stewart resented and tried to deflect by saying he had no right to punish him as he was not his own father. The 'family dance' was then enacted during arguments whereby the mother saw the conflict escalating between Stewart and his stepfather and stepped in before they could resolve anything. She believed that if she did not do this it would get out of hand and Stewart would be harmed. The stepfather thus felt that Stewart's mother did not trust him to deal with issues with the boy. She was placing him in a double bind where she counted on him to control Stewart but did not believe he did it properly. He was therefore very reluctant to get involved. Stewart's real father, whom Stewart visited every month, was involved in maintaining the problem since he claimed that 'Stewart is displaying many of my ex-wife's behaviours. I blame myself for allowing Stewart so much access to me over the years.' Thus, as he was asked to get involved to help Stewart, he had more and more doubts about getting involved at all and felt that he might have done too much over the years. Thus, the conflict between Stewart and his mum and stepfather was part of the way this family held together with Stewart's father, stepfather, mother and brothers and sisters all playing their part in maintaining the fight. The double bind situation which family members placed on each other whereby they asked for help and then disqualified the help they got from each other was clear to see. The outside agencies had compounded these issues because they put pressure on the system by being seen as suggesting that the parents' actions were, in some way, causing the problem, and the parents and Stewart then responded by the situation worsening and by him being removed.

It was clear from such a hypothesis based on their interaction as a family that the social worker's role had to deal with a whole variety of systems issues. First, the agencies involved in Stewart's problem were maintaining it through a variety of beliefs and behaviours – his teacher believed Stewart might need a psychiatrist to help him; the child guidance clinic believed he needed to be in a foster home because of the level of parental conflict which was causing him emotional damage; the residential home believed Stewart needed 'space' from his parents and so on. The parents believed that since his behaviour was worsening it was evident that it was not anything to do with them and, therefore, they did not have to 'own' the problem in any way and would not need to change their behaviour towards Stewart. Stewart was getting a considerable amount of attention for being bad and was being repeatedly asked what he believed should happen to him, which put him firmly in control over his own life and out of the remit of his parents. There had, therefore, to be a lot of work by the social worker in helping the agencies involved with Stewart to develop a common view about what Stewart and his parents needed. The agencies involved had to express their concern and agreed to an approach to Stewart's difficulties which strengthened parental authority and returned Stewart home to deal with his adolescent difficulties within his family system. The social work focus had to be on helping the mother and stepfather deal with Stewart's behaviour themselves without appealing to outside agencies, or to his natural father or arguing between themselves about how to tackle the problems. The rows between mum and Stewart were reframed as evidence of her deep emotional commitment to the boy and his behaviour was reframed not as sick or bad, but as the natural fight of an adolescent who was testing out the boundaries of parental control before leaving home. The stepfather was asked to suggest a variety of reasonable controls which he could use to stop Stewart losing his temper and lashing out at his mother and Stewart's mother was asked which of these she was prepared to let him use with Stewart. His ideas included holding him firmly while he calmed down and agreed to go to his room, but he was anxious that if he touched the boy, Stewart would report him to the police and he would be charged with harming him. This necessitated the social worker talking in some detail with the parents about the need for parents to control their children without shouting or hitting them or taking action in anger against them. There had to be some clear agreements between Stewart's mother and stepfather about how Stewart's behaviour would be controlled. When the stepfather physically restrained Stewart on one occasion after Stewart was returned home, Stewart said he felt that he had 'deserved it' for what he had said to his mum. The social worker concentrated on helping the parents control and set reasonable boundaries for the boy. Within a few months of his return, the family claimed that they did not need any further help. The social worker asked them whether, since they were experts in helping their adolescent boy to get under control, they would be willing to take part in some group sessions with other parents whose children were in care and who were struggling to re-establish control over their own adolescent children. They said they would be delighted to do this and Stewart's stepfather was particularly surprised that he should be seen as having anything to offer other parents with problems. They were reframed as experts in dealing with adolescent problems, not as failures as parents.

These two examples show two cases where the systems analysis of the problem tried to take more fully into account the social system of the client and to provide social work help based on minimal levels of intervention directed at those critical points of the systems functioning which was seen as maintaining the clients' difficulties. Examples of providing interventions which have a 'fit' with the ecology of the clients and reframes of pathology or Utopian ideas of 'cure' are evident in both situations.

Summary

Two case examples are given here: an elderly man, Mr M, and the 14-year-old boy Stewart and his family. In these examples, there is a systems analysis of the problems, a working hypothesis about how the agencies involved maintained the client's difficulties, and descriptions of how social work intervention was redesigned according to systems principles to provide a realistic resolution of those most problematic areas for the clients which threatened their ecology or social system.

CHAPTER 6

A Systems Approach to Social Work Management

> What would happen if deliberately, I disobeyed? I knew what would happen: nothing. Nothing would happen and the knowledge depresses me. I suppose it is just about impossible for someone like me to rebel any more and produce any kind of lasting effect. I have lost the power to upset things. I can no longer change my environment, or even disturb it seriously. They would simply fire and forget me as soon as I tried.
>
> Joseph Heller's manager, *Something Happened (1978)*

> What it comes to then, is that the opponents of a system cannot change it, while the system's friends do not want to. Thus no rational change is possible.
>
> Alvin W. Gouldner, *The Future of the Intellectuals and the Rise of a New Class (1979)*

The previous two chapters have provided principles and examples of the application of Bateson's systems ideas in social work practice. This chapter looks at their implications and provides principles for the management of social work organisations.

It is not intended to provide a detailed definition of management or to consider the many different roles and parts that social work managers play. Instead, the writers will provide a set of principles which can be used to guide the actions of managers in the often difficult and varied tasks they undertake. The writers will provide examples and illustrations of these principles being applied in a range of different areas of managerial activity. In the following chapter a full case study is used to illustrate an attempt to bring about major organisational change. Other examples cover using the principles in dealing with organisational problems, their use in teams and supervising practice, and their application in the implementation of new policies. The writers believe that these provide an essential basis for the development of a more ecological approach to management practice. At the heart of the ecological approach is the belief that within social work systems there is a wealth of untapped resources capable of resolving even difficult and long-standing problems. These resources lie in the creativity and resourcefulness of those in the system and the social work manager needs to create an environment in which such creativity can flourish rather than being squashed. This cannot be done through the increasing application of rules and regulations. The following principles are intended to help managers to enable their services to respond in new and creative ways.

Social work management has slowly absorbed the prevailing managerial culture. The early culture of social work developed within a bureaucratic model based on Weber – lines of accountability, rational structures, spans of control and so forth. (for a fuller discussion and critique of bureaucratic models of management see Morgan 1986). More recently, social work's managerial ideas have been absorbed from the new managerialism of market economics. This new culture pays some lip service to systems ideas and often statements are made by its adherents which suggest that the market economy is a self-regulating system. It would be entirely wrong to suggest that this has any parallel with the systems ideas proposed in this book. Bateson was clear that concepts such as circular causation had to be mastered before we are able to deal with our environment or even each other with respect (Bateson and Bateson 1988): 'Only if we do so will we be able to think seriously about the matrix in which we live, and only then will we recognise our affinity with the rest of that world and deal with it ethically and responsibly.'

Current managerial practices have clear linear models of causation and use crude target setting as the basis for action. The focus is on key performance indicators, national standards and quality measures, and the approach to achieving these various targets is usually based on providing ever-more prescriptive procedures and guidelines. Thus, on the introduction of the 1989 Children Act in England and Wales, the government not only changed the laws but also produced ten books of guidance for practitioners. Similar issues can be seen in the implementation of National Standards for work with offenders in Scotland and case management in Community Care. In area after area the introduction of a linear rationalistic approach to management can be seen and its hallmark is the stifling of creativity under the weight of procedures and guidelines. This trend is not limited to social work management and has been analysed by George Ritzer (1993) who has persuasively argued that it represents an approach to management epitomised by the McDonald's food chain and which he calls 'McDonaldisation'. McDonaldisation is a modern extension of Weber's theory of rationality to modern capitalist practices. For Weber (Ritzer 1993), formal rationality

> means that the search by people for the optimum means to a given end is shaped by rules, regulations, and larger social structures. Thus, individuals are not left to their own devices in searching for the best means of achieving a given objective. Rather, there exist rules, regulations and structures that either predetermine or help them discover the optimum methods.

McDonaldisation has a number of precursors, namely bureaucracy, scientific management and the assembly line. This approach is based, according to Ritzer, on the valuing of efficiency, calculability, predictability and control through the substitution of non-human for human technology. Whilst McDonaldisation can have the many benefits which Weber saw in bureaucracy, it is essentially dehumanising and leads to the irrationality that can be seen in queues for 'fast' food which is eaten in an environment in which even the chairs are designed to be uncomfortable enough to make customers eat quickly and move on. Ritzer suggests that Western culture has embraced this increasing 'rationalism' in most spheres. The evidence that McDonaldisation is being introduced in social work is all around. It can be seen in the performance indicators (efficiency); the increasing employment of accountants and sophisticated accountancy systems to cost individual care programmes in such fields as community care (calculability); Ritzer describes the way in which the autonomy of physicians is being increasingly constrained in order to 'impose more and more predictability' (1993); and a similar approach can be seen in the increasing regulations and controls being produced by central government for the practice of social workers in the fields of child care, child protection, the probation service and community care. The increasing regulation of all areas of social work is also an example of the increasing control of social work practice through an attempt to constrain the scope of human judgement through ever more rigid procedures.

The systems approach given here is different. It is built on the idea that within the organisation there is the capacity to adapt and change, and that the task of the manager faced with a problem is to tap into and encourage this ability. To do this he/she needs to be aware of the way that current approaches and responses are maintained by the unquestioned and often subconscious beliefs and presuppositions, which Bateson calls the epistemology, of the various participants in the organisation, as well as those in its environment. Whilst a rationalistic approach may bring more predictability and greater conformity, it is our contention that it will bring few real benefits for the users of social work services. Research (Thorpe and Bilson 1998) into the careers of children who have been involved in child protection investigations carried out by one of the writers provides a clear example of the way that the 'rational' approach to managing social work can create problems for families rather than offering them support. The approach to child protection in the agency studied was based on the government's prescriptive guidelines and was based on issuing extensive procedures which constrain the actions of social workers and the discretion of their managers when faced with an allegation of abuse. It has led to an increasing number of intrusive investigations as social workers and their managers alike conform to the prescriptive procedures. These investigations resulted, for the vast majority of children and families, not with the detection of abuse or injury but to an apology for the intrusion. The service moved from one concerned with the welfare of children to one which processed investigations and searched, usually in vain, for evidence. The response to the real problem of how to provide effective protection for children had, through the adoption of a rationalistic approach, led to a situation in which social workers acted to police unconventional or different patterns of child rearing.

The key principles for a more ecological approach to management are as follows:

- epistemology
- information
- adaptive interventions
- interconnectedness
- fit.

Epistemology

The mental framework people use to understand and interpret their world is a major factor in the development and maintenance of patterns of interaction in social systems. This is as true of the actors in social work as in other spheres. In earlier chapters we have discussed how Bateson used the term epistemology to refer to the set of beliefs and basic premises which underlie action and cognition. He suggests that epistemology specifies 'how particular organisms know, think and decide' (1980). This use of the term is broader than the traditional philosophical reference to the set of analytical and critical techniques that define boundaries for processing knowledge. Bateson suggests that a person's epistemology defines not only the way that the person perceives situations but also the possible actions (1973):

> In the natural history of the human being, ontology and epistemology cannot be separated. His (commonly unconscious) beliefs about what sort of world it is will determine how he sees it and acts within it, and his ways of perceiving and acting will determine his beliefs about its nature. The living man is thus bound within a net of epistemological and ontological premises which – regardless of ultimate truth or falsity – become partially self-validating for him.

In the writers' experience epistemologies concerning social work practice are developed interactionally. These sets of beliefs are evident at many different levels from national views to beliefs held within social work teams. And, as Bateson says above, they determine the ways that those who have them perceive and act. Pithouse's 1987 study of a child care team identified how the team's set of beliefs insulated them from change and shaped their actions in very powerful ways. Cohen identifies therapeutic language as part of the epistemology (in his words 'cognitive structures') of social work professionals (1985):

> The use of therapeutic language is not simple deception: 'many clients want help, virtually all professionals think they are providing it and sometimes they do!' We must not search for deliberate deception, but we must abandon the naive idea that words like 'pre-delinquent', 're-socialisation' or 'in need of care and protection' actually stand for particular persons, objects, behaviour or procedures. These words are symbols, elaborate cognitive structures that are full of ambivalence and ambiguity and that combine facts with beliefs, perceptions, emotions, habits and predictions.

An example of different epistemologies was seen by the writers when a group of police and social workers from Belgium visited a Scottish Sheriff's Court. A young man was convicted of a relatively minor offence and was sentenced to a short jail sentence. The young man was taken from the court to the cells to wait for his transfer to jail to serve his sentence. This was met by shock from the Belgian visitors who felt this was inhumane; how could someone be taken directly from court to prison for such an offence? In Belgium the man might have received the same sentence but he would have returned home and later, when a place in jail became available, he would receive a summons to serve his sentence. In this way he could prepare himself and did not come to court not knowing whether he would return home that night. The Scottish social workers and court staff could not believe such a system could be possible or that it would work. Until challenged by this difference they could not see that other ways of dealing with a prisoner under sentence might be possible.

The way that the epistemologies developed within teams can affect the practice of social work can be seen in one of the writers' recent studies of contact between parents and children in care (Barker and Bilson 1998; Bilson and Barker 1998). This study of five local authorities showed that within each local authority the patterns of contact differed, sometimes very significantly, between child care teams. These differences were often inexplicable in terms of the circumstances of the children and their families. For example, in one small local authority between 32 and 38 per cent of children in three teams had monthly contact with parents, whilst between 69 and 72 per cent of children in the other three teams had monthly contact. These findings were not explicable by differences in the circumstances of the children and families that are normally linked to lower levels of contact, such as length of time since being removed from home, the child's age, the reason the child entered care, the child's placement and so on. There was also nothing to show that these differences had anything to do with the resources available. This research took place after the implementation of the 1989 Children Act which stressed the need for social workers to focus on improving contact and which was accompanied within the authority by new procedures and training for all child care staff stressing the importance of contact. However, feedback from the teams showed that these differences were associated with differences in the beliefs about social work with children in care. The teams with low levels of contact believed that their role was one of 'rescuing' children from parents, whilst the other teams considered themselves to be working in partnership with parents.

Having identified these differences in epistemologies and their consequences for the services children and families receive, the task of effecting change is not necessarily easy. It is not the case that there is a simple 'correct' epistemology that can be offered as an alternative, nor that change can be achieved by simply pointing out to those involved the 'errors' in their approach. An example of this was encountered by one of the writers in the field of juvenile justice. He was involved in setting up a second team of workers to provide services for offenders in a small area of South Wales following a sudden increase in the use of care and custodial sentences. Research into the recommendations and contents of court reports on the children sentenced to custody and care showed how early involvement with the first 'preventive' project had been a major factor in the increased custodial sentencing, and yet the response of the agency was to set up a further 'preventive' project rather than to consider a change from the paradigm of 'prevention' (Bilson 1985, 1986). Having identified this problem, the common-sense approach would suggest that all that was necessary to bring about change was to present the research results and convince the staff, through logical argument, that their actions were not achieving the ends they desired. Indeed Nellis (1987), commenting on this research, came to the conclusion that 'all that needs to happen to avoid up-tariffing[1] is for magistrates (and [report] writers) to understand how preventive work and heavy end work differ, and to be willing to act on this understanding'. Whilst Nellis was correct in suggesting a change in understanding was needed, the task of achieving this apparently simple 'all that needs to happen' was a very complex one. The views of magistrates and report writers were based on deeply held assumptions and beliefs about offending, and within this framework of beliefs their actions were logical and rational. Achieving such a change in the way we see the world is not a simple matter of presenting data or giving the right sort of rational argument.

1 Up-tariffing is the rather ugly term coined for the notion that children may get a more intrusive sentence such as custody at an earlier stage for some reason other than their offending. The research which the author undertook looked at the reports social workers had written for the court appearance of offenders (called social enquiry reports – SERs) who had been sentenced to care or custody.

As Armstrong says of such a rational approach (1982):

> The rational approach is rational only for the change agent. For the changee, change seems *irrational.* Should we change important beliefs each time someone thrusts disconfirming evidence on us? It is not surprising that 'people are resistant to change.' The rational approach implies that the target of the change is irrational.

This issue of language and meaning is at the heart of social work and hence our expression of the need for epistemology to be addressed in the management of social work. The way we think about what is attempted is defined in advertisements, in descriptions of projects and in the language we use to describe our actions to clients, courts, other professionals, to each other and even in thinking about it ourselves. Cohen exhorts us to (1985):

> Listen carefully to social control talk: the inconsistent and varied words used by the workers, managers and ideologues of the system as they explain what they think they are doing and announce what they would like to do ... words neither 'come from the skies' (as Mao reminds us) nor can they be taken as literal explanations of what is happening. Nonetheless, we must listen to them very carefully. Words are real sources of power for guiding and justifying policy changes and for insulating the system from criticism ... leaving aside any putative 'implementation gaps' between rhetoric and reality, it is the rhetoric itself which becomes the problem.

In child care, for example, the term 'secure unit' is used as a euphemism for locked cells. This mystification allows those who have power (social workers, children's panel members, magistrates, etc.) to reinterpret the controlling nature of many of their actions as help or protection (the sexual activity of teenage girls being controlled by placing them in institutions, for example). This process does not stop at reconceptualising the reason for entry to care. Rather it continues and, for example, when a child responds to being in care by running away, committing offences or simply breaking the rules of the institution, the chances are that this will not be interpreted as a failure of the original attempt to 'help', but rather as a justification for the original intervention and of the need for more controlling measures. Forrester points out that the behaviour of social systems frequently runs against common sense or intuition and such 'counterintuitive' behaviour encompasses the belief systems of those involved. Thus in the example of secure units, beliefs based on the notion that statutory intervention is helping and in the best interests of children can become self-fulfilling since those children who successfully survive such intervention are seen as examples of success whilst the majority, whose situations worsen, are seen to justify the original belief about the need to intervene – a case of 'heads I win – tails you lose'. Similarly the use of the term 'secure training centre' in the 1994 Criminal Justice and Public Order Act to describe the locking up of children as young as 12 in institutions to provide punishment can be seen as a clue to the way in which those using the term may be hiding the oppressive nature of their actions.

> Dear Ms [name],
>
> I'm writing in connection with the investigation that was recently undertaken by PC [name], Child Liaison Officer, [town] Police and [name] a member of my staff, in respect of your daughter [name], aged 9 years.
>
> As you know, the reason why Social Services became involved was following the assault on [your child] by an unknown male on the evening of [date]. In line with this Authority's inter-agency Child Protection procedures we were informed of this by the Police. Subsequently under those same procedures members of my staff carried out a number of discreet background enquiries via other welfare professionals.
>
> Given therefore that there were [sic] no evidence of professional concern and that you had clearly acted to promote and protect [the child's] welfare, both before and after the incident, it has been agreed with the Register and Conference Service of this Department that we will take no further action in respect of this investigation.
>
> I have however asked [name], Social Worker, based at [neighbourhood] Children's Centre, [town] (telephone [number]) to contact you in the very near future, to see if you need any assistance or help either for yourself or [the child].

An example of what Cohen would have called social control talk can be seen in letters sent to families investigated under child protection procedures. The above example is drawn from a study carried out by one of the writers (Bilson and Thorpe 1998; Thorpe and Bilson 1998). The letter was one of many similar 'apologies' sent to families where an investigation had taken place and had not confirmed any abuse. The focus on investigation and an epistemology based on identifying evidence leads to a letter which is bureaucratic in tone, lacks humanity (here we have a family in which a child was assaulted in the street by a stranger being investigated himself) and is a clear example of the problems of the over-regulated and McDonaldised child protection system operating within the agency. It was no surprise that almost no families took up offers of help following receipt of such letters, even where the information available showed that some were in real need.

The implications of the principle of epistemology for managing social work fall into the following areas. The first concerns the way that our epistemologies shape the way that we conceptualise the work that we do and the actions that it is possible for us to take. This may be a good thing where it proves helpful to those to whom we provide services. But epistemologies can constrain our actions or even justify actions which are harmful to service users. Also by their very nature it is almost impossible to see their effects from within them. The inhumanity of a young man turning up in court for a minor offence not even knowing whether he would return home that night was not visible to workers in the Scottish Court mentioned above until they were confronted with visitors with different experiences and beliefs. Similarly, the teams which did not promote parental contact believed that they were acting in the best interests of their service users. As managers it is important to find ways to consider the impact of our epistemology on our practice. The following principles and the chapter on practice examples give ways to do this.

The second issue concerns the changing of epistemologies. As already mentioned this is no easy matter (although it also often happens spontaneously). As discussed in the earlier chapters the writers do not suggest that a new epistemology can or should be imposed. The following example shows how reflection on and the development of a new epistemology was undertaken with a group of staff responsible for tasking elderly people into residential care (for a fuller discussion of this example and a discussion of the theoretical framework used in it see Bilson 1996, 1997). A working party had been set up to examine criteria for entry to residential care for elderly people. Once these criteria were produced, a survey of recent entrants to residential care was undertaken which revealed that few, if any of them, met the new criteria (Booth and Bilson 1988). One of the findings of the survey was that a major factor in decisions to take people into homes was the social workers' belief that they were lonely, isolated and depressed in their own homes and that residential care would rescue them from this. Time and again, files included statements such as:

> Mrs P is beginning to become isolated and to feel lonely as she is without much company, especially in the evenings. She is very healthy and bright for her age but seems frail and delicate. She has no illnesses and has had

no recent illnesses. Apart from isolation, Mrs P has few problems and copes very well at home in spite of her age. She requires no special care so I would see the main aim of residential care for this lady would be to improve her quality of life by providing company and stimulation among her peers.

Mrs S has become very isolated since falling out with relatives who live nearby. She is now at risk from not eating and feeling depressed.

Mrs W suffers from communication problems following a stroke in 1983. She has had two falls and has been found wandering on one occasion. The main problem is her depression compounded by living alone.

In these cases the substantial research into the lack of interaction and high levels of depression in residents in old people's homes was not acknowledged, and residential care was being used for needs it could not meet. Rather than simply present the study to staff as a paper, it was decided that a two-day workshop would be held for fieldwork managers and other senior staff responsible for managing homes. The findings of research into old people's homes (Booth, Bilson and Fowell 1990) was presented as well as the results of the above survey. The managers were then given application forms and the files of another nineteen recent entrants to care and asked to decide whether they would now admit them. After consideration, the managers felt that fourteen should not have been admitted, in three cases there was insufficient information for a decision, and only two should have been admitted. The following day allowed managers to reconsider the function of old people's homes, to explore how they could ensure support in the community would be provided instead of admission, and to agree a plan for providing other members of staff with similar exercises and information. Like the family therapy technique of circular questioning, differences between beliefs about outcomes and the actual outcomes of social workers' actions were compared. The involvement of staff in the exercises meant that the research had the chance to have an impact on beliefs about social work in a way which enabled them to put their day-to-day knowledge of social work alongside information about patterns of outcome. It was aimed at helping them to reconsider and reflect on their epistemology. What emerged from the workshop was new ways of thinking about the situations of elderly people and the participants were involved in making significant changes to the services which the social work department provided.

Information

Bateson defines information as news of difference that makes a difference. For managers this idea can be seen to include the identification of differences and the process of creating news of those differences. A key idea in identifying differences is through pattern creation. Once patterns and differences have been discussed the section will go on to look at providing news of difference and, in particular, will look at the much misused concept of feedback.

In the discussion of epistemology above one way of getting to see the 'invisible' epistemologies which social workers were using was through the creation of patterns. In the example of the admissions to care of lonely old people, files were used for the initial study which identified an epistemology that sought to rescue people from their loneliness by taking them into residential care. Analysis of written communications can play a major role in identifying issues of epistemology through the creation of patterns. Reading files, reports, letters gives the reader a little more distance than he/she might achieve in talking to staff. It also allows the reader to create patterns across files such as those mentioned in this example. It needs to be said that, in suggesting that a report or file is a useful source of clues about epistemological issues, it is not being suggested that such documents contain truths about the situation. Like all communications they are situationally specific, written with a particular audience and a particular purpose in mind. However, the choice of language, the images and metaphors which the reader elicits from them, are an important source of information about the nature and types of beliefs the authors may have. It is important to read them in a way which tries to listen to the beliefs or images that underpin them and how they characterise those who are written about.

The very words being used also give clues, thus Cohen's (1985) exhortation for us to 'listen carefully to social control talk', as quoted earlier. Patterns may need to be compared in order to identify differences and a key way to do this is to use Bateson's idea of double description. For example, the pattern of reasons for admissions to homes for elderly people discussed above helped provide differences when it was compared with the department's policy (differences between expected reasons and actual reasons for entry); when it was compared with other patterns identified in research (differences between expected outcomes and outcomes about loneliness in the research); and when it was compared with the reasons social workers would say they used for admission (although the patterns were created from analysis of their files they were mainly invisible to the workers themselves).

Social work managers can build pattern identification into their work. For example, when asked to plan a group work programme for a child care team, one of the writers started by undertaking a review of social worker's child care cases. Using index cards and brief interviews with each social worker, key issues for each child on the workers' caseloads were recorded. The cards were then sorted into piles using different criteria, for example type of problem, age, gender, geographical area, school, and so on. In the course of this exercise the writer was able to identify a group of children all aged under ten coming from two small connected villages who had all either been sexually assaulted, or who exhibited sexualised behaviour towards other children. The writers then designed a programme to work with these children and their parents (Bilson and Ross 1981). This pattern had not been identified by individual workers or their seniors and only became visible because of the exercise. As a team leader it is possible to carry out similar exercises using information drawn from individual supervision sessions.

The second issue is creating news of difference and a major approach is in the use of feedback. The term feedback is frequently used by managers referring to the use of information without reference to its systems origins. From the early Macy conferences in the 1940s, feedback became the crucial issue to which the new science of systems theory addressed itself. Rosenblueth, Wiener and Bigelow (1968 [1943]) argued that 'all purposeful behaviour may be considered to require feedback'. Wiener's (Rosenblueth *et al.* 1968) definition of feedback, developed in 1945, is particularly relevant here:

> Feedback is a method of controlling a system by re-inserting into it results of its past performance. If those results are merely used as commercial data for the criticism of the system and its regulation, we have the simple feedback of the control engineer. If, however, the information which proceeds backwards from the performance is able to change the general method and pattern of performance, we have a process that may be called learning.

Much of the use of 'information' by social work managers remains at the level of simple feedback. Feedback which is aimed at changing the pattern of performance and geared to new learning in a system seldom occurs. From the discussion of epistemology above it will be seen that feedback aimed at enabling the organisation to learn needs to focus on the beliefs that underpin the actions of those in the organisation. At the level of simple feedback information systems are used to provide data on the degree to which the organisation is 'on course.' An example of this type of approach to feedback can be seen in the 'best value' initiative in the United Kingdom which stresses the monitoring of performance measures against cost; key performance indicators; provision of exception reports; and use of budgetary controls. Gareth Morgan (1986, 1993), the organisational theorist, discusses how the use of information systems in this way can actually discourage change and innovation, disabling the organisation's ability to adapt to changes in its environment. He suggests that this is particularly true of bureaucratic organisations where the focus on performance goes along with an inability to question the epistemology or to challenge 'basic norms, policies and operating procedures' (1986).

For example, information systems are frequently being used as part of the standardisation of the services provided in home care. Contracts specify in great detail the performance tasks required of the carer and these are monitored through time sheets. In this way managers can know the extent to which these contractual services are being achieved, but it does not challenge whether this contractual service is what the service user really wants and needs. Information from service users gives a much better indication of what is wanted and how far this differs from the McDonaldised service being specified. What service users value is the personal contact, the humanity and care they receive from 'their' home carer. The following quote from a satisfied customer, one of many similar comments, typifies this: 'She has the patience of a saint and no job is too big or too small... No doubt I am a lucky person to have such a great home help' (Ross 1999a) The rationalistic approach to managing home care is currently seen in many other social work service areas and leads to services being reduced to their lowest common denominators with the danger that the real value of the service is lost.

Adaptive interventions

People wishing to bring about change in social work organisations or practice often feel much the same as Heller's manager quoted at the beginning of the chapter. They feel they have little or no influence and are daunted by the sheer size and weight of the organisation. Margaret Power (in Walker and Beaumont 1985), talking about the probation officer's role in the juvenile court, sums this up thus: 'There are dangers for those on the margins of powerful institutions. They tend to draw you in, take you over, incorporate you, write you off as an irrelevance.' On the other hand, where social work managers attempt to bring about change, it is often notable that the new policy, service, procedure or working practice is absorbed or incorporated in a way which leads to little alteration in the operation of the system. One problem for those wishing to initiate change is that the eye is drawn to those parts of the system where intervention will have little or no effect. Forrester (1972) sums this up as follows:

> Social systems are inherently insensitive to most policy changes that people select in an effort to alter the behaviour of the system. In fact, a social system tends to draw your attention to the very points at which an attempt to intervene will fail.

The provision of feedback described above enables social work systems to adjust and change through changes in epistemology. However, the generation of information about patterns in social work systems also enables those involved in a system to modify responses in order to produce better outcomes for consumers. One approach to this is for managers to develop adaptive interventions. An adaptive intervention aims to make small changes to the current patterns in order to change the way it operates. Often these small changes can lead to major changes in the outputs of the system. This can be illustrated by an example from work in England with young offenders. An adaptive intervention was developed in an agency where, in the previous year, the court sentenced nine young people to custodial sentences because they failed to complete their attendance centre order and were taken back to court for non-compliance by the police. This was ascertained through an analysis of the court statistics for that year. Following the identification of this pattern discussions were held between the police and the youth justice team and an agreement reached that, if a child failed to report to his attendance centre on two consecutive occasions, the police would follow their usual procedure and issue a standard warning followed by a visit. If the child still did not attend the police would contact the youth justice team before instigating breach proceedings to see if it could ensure compliance with the order. This resulted in 15 young people being referred in the following year, most of whom, with a little help, completed their attendance centre orders successfully following intervention by the team. This help sometimes took the form of practical assistance such as arranging transport to the centre. In the somewhat unusual case of one boy who was asthmatic and generally fearful of the physical exercises at the centre, the police agreed not to insist on full attendance, and in the case of another boy who was frightened of being bullied, the worker attended with him to help him complete the order. No one received a custodial sentence because of breach of an attendance centre order and the police were very pleased that 'something was being done' for the children who had difficulty completing their orders.

What is particularly relevant in this example is that it did not seek to bypass the efforts made by the police to enable the children to complete their attendance centre orders. It only came into operation at the point where the usual way of dealing successfully with the problem had failed. It was, therefore, a real 'addition' to the system's operation. In that sense, it 'goes with' the ecology of the system and complements the system's way of dealing with problems, rather than trying to change large sections of the system.

The small change in process had major effects in the youth justice system as a whole. It had a knock-on effect of increasing confidence in the attendance centre order as an alternative to custody, since the police and the courts knew that the order would be completed. The scheme also gave some measure of protection, built into the system's operation, for a young person receiving an attendance centre order, who would not receive a custodial sentence by default through the breaching of their order. It thus gave social workers and probation officers more confidence to recommend an attendance centre order as a relevant alternative to custody in difficult cases where compliance might become a problem.

Interconnectedness

One of the features of natural systems to which systems theory draws attention is their interconnected nature. Intervention in one area of a social work system will always affect the other components of that system. So, for example, a social work department attempting to restrict significantly the use of residential care in Scotland will affect the behaviour, responses and belief systems of the children's panel, the reporter, the police, the education department, the child guidance service and any other significant bodies that operate within the child care arena. The nature of the interconnectedness of the various different components is hard to define. Katz and Kahn (1966) said:

> Social structures are essentially contrived systems that are made of men, and are imperfect systems. They can come apart at the seams over night, but they can also outlast by centuries the biological organisms which originally created them. The cement that holds them together is

> essentially psychological rather than biological. Social systems are anchored in their attitudes, perceptions, beliefs, motivations, habits and the expectations of human beings.

It is perhaps not surprising, therefore, that any significant change in one part of the system will create tension and pressure within the system between the various elements that make it up and within the elements themselves. Systems deal with the forces within them for change and stability by seeking a new order. As Kast and Rosenzweig (1972) say: 'These counteracting forces will often create tensions, stresses and conflicts which are natural and should not be considered as totally disfunctional.'

The experience of changing the services provided by a social work department is often accompanied by conflicts, tensions and stresses between the department and other agencies as well as within the agency itself. This can be with any other agency in the system, or with many or all of the various agencies. Conflicts are part of the system's response to new inputs as the process of accommodation to change is embarked on, just as a natural environment adapts when one species become stronger and other species will change their position in the pecking order to create a new balance. It is important when trying to bring about changes in social systems to encourage the process of accommodation to the new input, rather than trying to maintain the dominance of one part of the system over the other. This is the major way in which the levels of conflict can be reduced during periods of change. The input changes the whole system, even if that process is begun by changing one part. This means that one part of a system must not claim the credit for producing changes even if the impetus for changes does come from one element of the system. As Bateson (Bateson and Bateson 1988) explained:

> Let us now consider what happens when you make the epistemological error of choosing the wrong unit: you end up with the species versus the other species around it or versus the environment in which it operates. Man against nature. You end up, in fact, with the Kaneohe bay polluted, Lake Erie a slimy green mess and 'let's build better atom bombs to kill off the next door neighbours'. There is an ecology of bad ideas, just as there is an ecology of weeds, and it is characteristic of the system that basic error propagates itself. It branches out like a rooted parasite through the tissues of life, and everything gets into a rather peculiar mess. When you narrow down your epistemology and act on the premise 'what interests

> me is me, or my organisation, or my species', you chop off consideration of the other loops of the loop structure.

Bateson continually emphasised that, because change comes from within the ecology of systems, it is vital to take on board the ecological consequences of every new input and to look at the meaning for the system of those changes. Thus, in trying to change social work responses, it is vital to address the epistemological questions not just about why the change is necessary, but also about what social work intervention is about and what it can realistically achieve. These issues cannot be ignored if the ecology of the social work system is to be able to adjust to the changes rather than disqualify them. The changes themselves must become part of the wider system's ecology – not just one part of the system trying to influence the operation of the other part by the exercise of power. Introducing a change in the social work response to clients in the social work agency will influence all parts of the system which will accommodate to that change. The social work agency will itself be affected by the system's accommodation and is thus not in a position to force change on the wider system. This notion of 'power' to influence the system is rejected by Bateson as 'a myth' (1980):

> After all, the man 'in power' depends on receiving information all the time from outside. He responds to that information just as much as he 'causes things to happen' ... He must then trim what he says to this information and then again find out how they are responding. It is an interaction and not a lineal situation.

Thus, if changes are 'owned' by one element in a system – for example, if reductions in children entering residential care are repeatedly attributed to one element of the system (e.g. the social work policy for children and families is linked only to better social work practice, or to the director of social work's decision to close residential establishments, or to a particular child care consultancy) then that perpetuates the notion that one part of the system retains power over the other parts. It will mean that the inevitable tensions around the subsystem boundaries will continue to cause difficulties and may, indeed, escalate. As Bateson reminds us, it is only through interactions that systems develop. To assume that one part has dominance over the actions and beliefs of other parts of the system always leads to disastrous outcomes. Keeney (1983) sums up this issue in relation to the tasks of therapy thus:

> A therapist who sees himself as a unilateral power-broker or manipulator is dealing with partial arcs of cybernetic systems. Such a position threatens the recursively structured biological world in which we live. Only wisdom, that is 'a sense or recognition of the fact of circuitry' ... can safely and effectively deal with eco-systems ... intervention strategies that do not consider the ecology of the problems they attempt to alter will help breed higher orders of pathology. We are, therefore, responsible for contextualising our techniques, whether they belong to medicine, education, engineering or psychotherapy.

Changes, therefore, cannot be owned within the system by one part of it, or held on to as the achievements of one element over the rest. Selvini-Palazzoli *et al.*'s (1978) experience, discussed in Chapter 3, of the way the referring agent in therapy disqualifies change by ensuring that the problems are maintained, not solved, has direct relevance if positive changes in social work systems are not to be disqualified by the wider system. The team had to find ways of attributing any change to the referrer and not to their therapeutic methods. Any successes in changing social work systems should be attributed to all parts of the systems endeavour. The 'wholeness' of the system has to be worked with and its ecology recognised, following Varela (1976): 'unless you confront the mutualness, the closure of a system, you just lose the system.'

Fit

The techniques from family therapy such as circular questioning, using a reflecting team, and hypothesising can be adapted to the particular situation of management of an organisation. However, such adaptation requires care and attention to the differences between families and organisations as well as between therapy and management. Whilst Imber-Black (1986) provides examples of successfully using circular questioning techniques as part of her work in 'human-service-provider systems', Borwick, an organisational consultant, describes a series of consultations in which he worked with Boscolo and Cecchin from the Milan group. These consultations used standard hypothesising and circular questioning techniques with a number of management teams. He states (1986): 'What was patently clear was that applying family systemic techniques without modifying them for the conditions of a business organisation had proved unsuccessful.'

A key issue identified by Borwick in this application of the Milan approach in an organisation was the family therapist's focus on pathology.

These concerns are 'a violation of the business system rules and send shock waves through the system'. It is here that 'fit' becomes an important concept. The manager has to respect the nature of the organisation even where this is seen as part of the problem. For example, in a hierarchical organisation an ecological approach would seek to reduce the use of power and encourage more cooperative approaches. Whilst the hierarchical nature of the organisation may be seen as central to this problem, acting in ways which ignore the current state of the organisation is likely to lead to rejection of the attempts to bring about change.

An example of working to gain fit can be seen at a conference held by an agency in which one of the writers and a colleague had carried out research into child care practice (Bilson and Barker 1994, 1995). The research had indicated what the writer considered to be rather depressing findings about the quality of the practice in the area investigated. On arrival, the writer and his colleague were informed that the audience were angry with, and had been hostile to, the previous speaker who had also presented research which was critical of the practice of the staff in the agency. Over coffee they were told that they were going 'to be in for a rough time, particularly with the results you are going to present which are much more critical of practice than the last speaker's'.

In this situation it was crucially important to find a fit with the audience. This involved a complex process where, whilst speaking to the audience, the writer was also carefully looking for signs of their response and being aware of his feelings and using these indicators to guide and adapt his approach. It is difficult to describe this process and the danger is that, taken out of this context, the description sounds trite or, worse still, cold and manipulative. However, the writer will attempt to describe certain aspects which he, on reflection, felt were important in this attempt to provide an ecological intervention aimed at changing the practices which seemed to him to be damaging children.

The writer started by thanking the audience for their participation in the research and the efforts they had made to return the completed questionnaires quickly. He talked about the fact that, although now working in an 'ivory tower', he was first and foremost a social worker and his interest was not in doing research for its own sake but in the practice of social work. He also stressed the limited nature of the research and the need to be wary of drawing too-firm conclusions based on what was a limited study and joked about some of the shortcomings in the design. By this time some of the initial tension and resistance that the writer sensed in the audience had started to dissipate and they were laughing at the jokes and so on. One of the main points of the presentation and a key pattern identified in the research was that many siblings in care were placed in separate placements and then lost all contact with one another.

Having 'joined' with the audience, the writer started to present a brief outline of the findings. When he came to the results concerning siblings he said how these had worried him. He talked about the importance of sibling relationships; how they are likely to be the longest lasting relationship that anyone is likely to have. He then described a situation in which he had been involved with two sisters who had supported each other through terrible abuse at home, had been separated in care and lost touch. He described the situation in detail, describing the way that one of them left care and the other, several years later, continued to blame herself for their separation. He described the pain of this for the girl and the joy that came when these estranged sisters were eventually brought back together. He shared with the audience his strong feelings about this, whilst being careful not to blame the social workers involved in the case. The audience appeared moved by the story and he then helped them to reconsider the figures about the numbers of separated and 'lost' relationships through the image of the pain of separation of these two sisters. A similar approach was taken to the findings regarding the low level of contact between children in care and their parents.

At the end of the talk there were many animated questions about the findings and their implications and conversations about what might be done. The writer and his colleague were applauded and thanked for their presentation. Whilst no firm conclusion can be drawn about the effects of this single presentation, and it would be wrong to make strong claims, a repeat of the initial study found that there was a significant increase in the proportions of children having contact with their parents and with their separated siblings. This was in contrast to the results of a second survey in a neighbouring agency where it had proved impossible properly to engage staff in considering the results.

In this intervention the key elements were the need to gain a fit with the audience through engaging the emotions of the audience; using patterns created from the results of the research to provide news of difference; and the attempt to help the audience to see the ethical implications by using an example to show how the 'facts and figures' might represent human tragedies. In describing this intervention, as in other examples, it is hard not to speak as if the reality seen by the writer through his understanding of the research was *the* reality, and that the process was one of winning the audience over to a particular point of view. However, even in this situation where dialogue with the audience is limited by the formal nature of a presentation, the speaker can become tuned in to the non-verbal feedback from the audience and respond to it in ways that shape and inform the intervention. The writer has presented this particular piece of research in a number of forums and each 'conversation' has been different, and often his own views of the meaning and significance of the findings have changed during the discussion. Gaining fit is not a unilateral action applied to an audience, but requires all parties to join a conversation and be open to the possibility of change if they are to co-construct new meaning.

Summary

This chapter identifies key principles for creative social work management. It suggests that changing social work organisations to produce better outcomes for their clients requires a fundamental reassessment of our beliefs about management. The principles outlined above should lead to management practice which moves from the rationalistic approach to one which encourages and supports creativity and which values both staff and service users. The following systems principles offer a way of considering such a new approach to social work management.

Epistemology

Social workers and managers develop sets of assumptions which shape how they see situations and the actions they can take. These assumptions are often invisible and may maintain oppressive or poor practice. Managers need to develop ways of considering the epistemologies in their teams and agencies and where necessary helping staff to change them.

Information

Managers need to find ways of identifying patterns in the practice of their agencies and to provide feedback which encourages new responses to the changing environment of the social work services they provide.

Adaptive interventions

Adaptive interventions aim to introduce small changes to the current pattern of practice aimed at changing the way it operates. These small changes can disrupt the current patterns leading to major changes in service outcomes.

Interconnectedness

The interlinked nature of organisations must be borne in mind so that there is an understanding that changes which affect other parts of the social system can cause conflicts and tensions between agencies and organisations linked to, and affected by, that change. These issues have to be worked with rather than avoided or denied. This section suggests some ways in which this might be achieved.

Fit

Interventions must be developed which have a 'fit' with the social work system. Techniques from family therapy need to be carefully adapted for use in organisations and managers need to be sensitive to the culture of the organisation or team in order for their interventions to be effective.

CHAPTER 7

Social Work Management

Systems Case Studies

> The pursuit of 'policy' was central to our study. Any naive ideas we may have had at the outset that it could be swiftly identified and understood and that its effects would be readily traceable in the actions of operational staff were very quickly dispelled. Grasping 'policy' was a matter of trying to capture something that was multidimensional, constantly moving and, furthermore, something that appeared ghostly and insubstantial in outline and detail.
>
> Packman, Randall and Jacques, *Who Needs Care (1986)*

The previous chapter proposed a number of principles to be considered when attempting to adopt a systems approach to social work management. This chapter describes three examples of this approach. The first discusses a systems approach to helping a manager deal with a particular and difficult problem. The second is actions in a Scottish social work department to bring about changes in its responses to children and families at risk or in trouble. The third example relates to the somewhat unusual managerial approach to evaluating, developing and changing the home help service in a social work department. These examples are being put forward not as models for others to slavishly follow, nor because the strategies being described were uniquely successful in bringing about positive change. What they raise are some of the issues encountered when applying systems ideas to real life managerial situations.

Case study 1

The first case study concerns the use of information to deal with a problem in an organisation. In this case the managerial action is not focused directly on the provision of services, but on the internal 'politics' of the organisation. The issue was raised by a home help manager at an in-service course for managers in a social work agency which was led by one of the writers. The course was similar to that described in the next chapter and was aimed at giving managers skills in creating patterns from management data and in line with Bateson's definition of information. The course also focused on presenting the patterns in ways that 'make a difference'. In addition to data drawn from the agency's client information system, participants were encouraged to bring along information which they regularly handled in their jobs. This included client information as well as budget statements and budget monitoring reports. It should be noted that whilst managers in social work are increasingly expected to be able to use information systems, few have had even basic training in this area.

The participants on the course were asked to share a problem that they had in the use of information. A home help manager was concerned about absence monitoring (the collection of information on the proportion of staff being absent due to sickness in a given period). The agency was facing a possible overspend on its budget and senior managers were looking for savings. At the same time figures had been published which showed that the social work agency had a particularly high rate of staff absences. A prominent local politician had raised the heat on this issue in the media berating the senior managers for not dealing with this problem whilst they were looking to cut services to make budget reductions.

In view of this background it was not surprising that the management had decided to scrutinise this element of expenditure. All departmental managers were given instructions on dealing with this problem; information was provided on the crude rate of absences split down to the level of individual budget holders; and where this reached a particular threshold the responsible manager was called in to headquarters to be interviewed by the director and other senior managers.

The home help manager had been called to an interview which was to take place after the course. She raised this as a problem she would like to focus on and brought along the details of her staff absences. She had taken over the management of the service six only months earlier and felt that she had done a lot to improve things. However, looking at the overall figures that were being used by the senior managers it appeared that the problem had become worse during the time she had been in charge.

Thus the problem she faced was how to deal with the 'interview' which, from rumour in the department (which may or may not have been true but was believed), would effectively consist of her being given little chance to explain and being dressed down for failure to take the issue on. The senior management of the department had recently had industrial action taken by managers focusing on a restructuring which had initially been dealt with in a very authoritarian way and the approach to the problem of sickness leave also suggested that they were operating within an epistemology based on power – i.e. that problems could be solved by issuing directives and taking managers who did not comply 'to task'. Any attempt at dealing with the home help manager's position needed to take this into account and should also be aimed at helping to move them from this epistemological position.

The home help manager was understandably nervous at the thought of having to defend herself in an interview as a relatively new and junior member of staff. Also it was difficult for her to see the situation other than from within the same epistemology. As Bateson suggests, the difficulty in bringing about changes in epistemology is not simple (1973):

> At this point you discover to your horror that it is exceedingly difficult to get rid of the error, that it is sticky. It is as if you had touched honey. As with honey, the falsification gets around; and each thing you try to wipe off on gets sticky, and your hands still remain sticky.

On discussing the situation with her it became clear that she had been taking the issue of staff absence seriously. Fortunately she had collected her own information on staff absences and from this it was possible to create a more complex pattern which carried a very different meaning. The figures showed that the overall pattern of absence amongst her staff was low, with the exception of two home helps who had been absent for the majority of the time she had been in charge. Both these staff members had had poor sickness records over a long period under the previous manager who had taken no action. Since taking over she had taken formal action following the procedures of the agency and the contracts of both staff members were soon to be ended due to their inability to carry out their duties. This pattern thus showed her to be managing the problem. She had also set up support systems for her other home carers, arranging group meetings and supervision to provide them with support and reduce the risk of unnecessary stress.

Whilst this data gave her a good case there was a real danger that if the managers acted as it was predicted it may not be heard. She had to get the opportunity to present it and to do it in a way which would make a difference.

As well as feeling worried at being called to the meeting she was also angry that she was being 'punished' for a problem which she had taken seriously and which she was close to solving. She also felt powerless because of her position. In addition, having to pay the staff during their absence had meant that she had been forced to reduce the service in her area to keep within her budget. This was in contrast to some other areas which were over-spending. There was the danger that, even if she could convince the senior managers that she had solved the sick-leave problem, she would still face a budget reduction on the basis that she could continue to provide the same level of service once the two absent staff were no longer employed, thus saving their wages.

Any strategy thus had to deal with the problems of the epistemology of power. In the first instance this meant helping the home help manager to move out of this as it left her feeling 'powerless'. Drawing parallels between what the senior managers were trying to do and her own actions in combatting the absence records of her own staff helped her to reassess the situation and providing a new framework for understanding the situation (the systems framework from this book) gave her the ability to see different options for action and to devise a strategy.

If her input was to be heard she would have to get a fit with the senior managers. This was difficult because of her feelings at being summoned there. The approach she decided to use was what in family therapy is called a 'yes and ...' approach. She would agree with the managers at the seriousness of the current situation regarding sick leave in her area. This would give her the opportunity to join with them and show her genuine concern at the problem. She would then show how the problem was worse than they thought because the reduced service caused by the absences was negatively affecting the lives of service users, increasing their risk of entry to residential care which they did not want, and would lead to greater expenditure by the agency. As discussed in earlier chapters, trying to address problems of epistemology through logical argument is unlikely to succeed. It was important to engage them in reflecting on the impact of their actions. She needed to engage them emotionally before giving more rational arguments. To do this she would use case examples demonstrating the very real impact of her decisions to temporarily reduce service levels on service users. She would then give some brief figures demonstrating the pattern identified in the sick leave and showing how this would be resolved in the next monitoring period. The important thing here was to present in a way which had an impact. As is often the case with managers in such situations, the home help manager wanted to present very detailed information, but she had limited time and it was important to get her point across quickly, stressing the differences between her analysis and the crude figures being used for monitoring. The writer helped her to devise a tightly focused presentation which could quickly demonstrate the issues. In this way she would not only put across her own case but also expose issues about an approach based on crude information.

Following her 'interview' the home help manager reported that things had gone well. Not only had she been praised for the work she had done on monitoring, but there had also been no cuts in her budget allowing her to reinstate the precious level of service.

Using a systems approach had enabled the home help manager to deal successfully with a situation in which she had previously felt powerless and oppressed. The example shows the importance of avoiding being drawn in to view problems through the epistemology of power and how systems approaches can help managers to look for different ways of tackling difficult situations.

Case study 2

The next example occurred when an agency tried to bring about change in its responses to children and families at risk and in trouble. It began when the agency concerned adopted a policy statement 'Services for Children and Families'. This policy stressed voluntarism – the principle that no statutory order should be used with families and children if they were prepared to work without any element of compulsion. The aim of the policy was to reduce the need for families to have their children taken into care and, where families needed advice or guidance, to organise services in a way which reduced the need for statutory involvement by, for example, providing welfare rights advice on financial problems. Where children were to come into care the focus of the policy was on short-term, planned services preferably provided within families rather than in institutions.

This policy statement was drawn up following a series of meetings chaired by a senior manager involving over 200 staff from all parts of the department. At the time of these meetings, the number of children in residential homes had been falling for a few years and closures were planned on the basis that the homes were less than half full.

It is worth mentioning for readers unfamiliar with the Scottish children's hearing system that control over entry to care and over placements of children who are in care, where they have entered through the children's hearing system, are not at the social worker's discretion. The children's hearing controls placements in care and length of stay, and once on an order this is reviewed at the hearing which continues to decide what happens to the child. Whilst social workers make recommendations, the power lies with the members of children's panels for this large proportion of children.

The strategy described was not planned from a neat beginning following the adoption of the policy. Rather, it evolved as issues became identified and as changes occurred over time. Looking back, there appear to be common themes but these were not always apparent at the time. Further, the example focuses on the actions of managers in the social work department. This is because of the viewpoint of the writers, and is also determined by the nature of this chapter with its focus on organisational change. It is important to remember that this is just one punctuation of the sequence of events. The changes in social work provision would not have been possible without the very considerable efforts of individual social workers and other actors in the system, including children's hearing members, Reporters to the children's hearings, staff of the education department, police and, most importantly, the children and families themselves. From many of these perspectives, the events described will be differently perceived and have different significance. The description that follows is thus a partial one.

At the time this policy was adopted, there was little information available to guide practice. It was even unclear how many children were in care. The first part of the strategy was to collect information about what was happening to children and families and to ensure that these results were made widely available to provide feedback on the operation of the system.

A number of studies were undertaken which confirmed the applicability of external findings about the instability of care placements, the high rate of problematic behaviour (such as absconding and offending), the poor prognosis in terms of education, future offending, likelihood of custodial experience and diminishing family contact. This is not to say that these factors were present in all cases, nor that there were not children for whom removal from home was the most appropriate action. Indeed, Bilson and Thorpe in their detailed study of research in the agency state (1988):

> There is little doubt that for some children, especially younger children in short stay voluntary care, child care systems can provide many benefits

> and give valuable services to families. Long term compulsory care is quite a different matter, it is clear that there are formidable difficulties in this area.

There was, however, evidence of the type which led the DHSS to state that social work departments find 'it difficult to provide good enough parenting for the individual child in care' and for them to suggest that 'a revolution in managerial thinking' is necessary as 'the situation is undoubtedly serious because the gap between aims and achievement in the child care service is still distressingly wide' (1983). The results of studies into children in care were presented to staff in the department. The gathering and use of information is a central part of a systems approach. Attempts were made to ensure that the results were presented to a wide range of audiences and that, whilst they were presented in a way which had a 'fit' with the particular audience, they also provided news of difference about outcomes of care. For example, one study showed that a high proportion of children attending a residential school reoffended or, in the case of those not offending prior to being placed in the school, commenced offending with a high proportion going on to secure units or custody. For social workers, one of the surprising findings was that most children were placed in the school following a social work recommendation for those placements.

An external consultant was engaged to assist in the realisation of the policy. The benefits of this not only included specialist expertise, but also provided a viewpoint from someone who was not directly involved in the system. During the consultancy, further research was carried out that allowed comparisons between children who entered care before and after the adoption of the policy (Bilson and Thorpe 1988).

Another element of the strategy focused on report writing. It has been mentioned earlier that this is an important issue to address since, in choosing to include and exclude information and in giving explanations for behaviour and possible social work plans, the report writer exposes beliefs and understandings about child care. It is these epistemological issues which are the focus for attention in a systems approach. The series of workshops for managers and later for social workers focused on these issues by providing alternative frameworks through the presentation of theory and research findings and, more importantly, through exercises focused on the contents of reports. All reports submitted in a three-month period were collected and analysed by managers. This enabled identification of patterns in a way that was not normally possible because of the focus on individual cases. It became clear that there was an absence in most cases of social work plans. There were also generally negative comments in the majority of the reports about the child's family, and a lack of information on the reason the child and family were appearing before the children's panel. From these exercises, guidance for reports was created and developed in workshops followed by a trial of the guidance by social workers, more feedback from managers and, after consultation inside and outside the department, the adoption of the guidance which was then presented at further seminars. The analysis of the reports and the presentation of the new guidance allowed many opportunities to provide feedback and re-examine understandings about the operation of the child care system and the social workers' roles in it.

Children's panels have to decide whether compulsory measures of care are in the best interest of the child. The issues of compulsory and voluntary measures were the focus of much discussion and part of the guidance on reports addressed this, helping to clarify how the social worker assessed the necessity of compulsory measures of care in order to make a recommendation to the hearing. This approach, involving staff in analysing reports, is similar to certain action research methods. However, the emphasis on epistemology is most significant in systems terms.

Turning now to the effects of these interventions it has to be said that the introduction of the policy for children and families, which was linked to substantial closures of residential places for children in children's homes, was accompanied by a significant, and almost immediate, worsening of relationships with other agencies involved in the children's hearing system. This was particularly so with members of the children's panel, the education department and the child guidance service. With the social work department's continuing emphasis on preventing young people being removed from home, the conflicts escalated and were evident at every level of the systems operation, from corporate policy planning to individual discussions in children's panels about particular young people in difficulties. The following two extracts illustrate the level and degree of conflict very well. The first is an extract from a newspaper reporting the introduction of a joint statement from the Director of Social Work and the Director of Education for dealing with 'provisions for youngsters with social, emotional and educational difficulties'. This report was written two years after the original publication of the social work department's policy for children and families. The two departments' positions and the degree of tension on their 'boundaries' was very evident even in the press reporting of the discussion of this.

Council's Care Policy Comes Under Attack

... Regional Council's policy on community care for children with social, emotional and educational difficulties was attacked, yesterday by Councillor T... D..., chairman of the Region's Education Department. Mr D, warning members of a joint subcommittee on provision for children with such difficulties, said the Council were travelling 'too far too fast'.

'Haste must be made more slowly,' he said, emphasising that he believed in the philosophy of care in the community.

The subcommittee meeting had before them, a joint report outlining the Region's proposed policy for tackling the problem of provision for youngsters with social, emotional and educational difficulties ... the document stresses the need for cooperation between the two departments involved ... Mr D then expressed his fears. 'It was necessary for this joint report to be produced,' he said, adding that the problem facing the Council was a 'multi-disciplinary challenge and not a challenge to one department in this authority'.

'I hope one general aspect of this joint report will be that, as of today we will set up a means of monitoring, analysing and evaluating whether or not this policy requires to be amended or whether it is working efficiently'.

Mr D said later that he believed the policy of care in the community was the correct one.

However, in terms of implementation, the Council would have to make haste more slowly than had been the case in the last year to 18 months.

'By that means we can secure a caring policy which recognises that the total community requires to be satisfied that the provision we are hoping to make does not, in fact, threaten the community itself by being over-hasty,' he explained.

The Director of Social Work said, 'we have in ... achieved a tremendous reduction in numbers of children in care.

The strength of the Region's policy has been to keep children with their families.'

However, the Director of Education then told Councillors that the policy 'isn't working satisfactorily', and that the success suggested by the Director of Social Work 'might be open to question'.

> The subcommittee agreed to call for further examination of the matter.

The second example was a letter written from a psychologist to the reporter to the children's hearing system about a child called Jane, to decide on her 'best interests'. The subject of the report, Jane, was a 15-year-old girl who had been expelled from her third high school placement.

The second paragraph of the psychologist's report read:

> Whilst not wishing to suggest for a moment that the Education Authority has really appropriate resources for Jane in the current circumstances, it is my firm opinion that, whatever were the complex family issues at the beginning, the major part of Jane's difficult situation is both directly and indirectly a consequence of the Region's Social Work Department's apparent inability or unwillingness to countenance anything other than the official interpretation of their child care policy which might be paraphrased as 'a family situation is, will and always will be the best for all children at all times'. The actual child care policy document does acknowledge that, for some children at certain times, residential placement even outwith the Region (!) may be necessary, but the apparent intimidatory pressures applied within the Department to coerce fieldworkers into compliance have been equally as strong and successful as the denials given to my service's Senior Officers by the Senior Officers of the Social Work Department that this is not so ... Jane has been treated like a pawn and I find it difficult to see how the Social Work Department's policy, as implemented, has actually served Jane, rather it has done her disservices on more than one occasion because fieldworkers, whatever their real professional judgements about Jane's needs and best interests, have felt threatened enough to try to follow the Departmental diktat rather than the actual policy as written ... I trust these and other views can be aired at an early panel.

These tensions clearly affected the interactions within the system in terms of policy, resources and individual children. Such tensions and conflicts are part of the system's response to new input as it accommodates to change. In this case, the myth of power was raised as changes were deemed to be too fast and were attributed to the social work department's implementation of its policy and thus profoundly rejected by the other important agencies in the system. In such situations, the interconnectedness of the system needs to be addressed.

Another phenomenon in systems experiencing this type of change is that perceptions of the operation of the system can become distorted. This may be because of the introduction of news of difference or because the changes have meant that events which were previously everyday ones have been attributed a new meaning. These misconceptions often take the form of beliefs that the trend of changes is going in the wrong direction. For example, during the changes in the agency, social workers and their managers believed that many children's hearing decisions were going against recommendation with the effect that the numbers of children in care must be increasing. This misconception was due both to the increased focus on children at risk of entry to care as well as the changes to recommendations for voluntary social work support. Despite clear evidence to the contrary, this misconception continued to hold sway for a considerable period. Elsewhere in the system some children's panel members believed, as did the psychologist quoted above, that social workers were being coerced into making recommendations against care even though social workers attending panels denied this. Such myths can, in the writers' experience, be a substantial force against change and are difficult to counteract because of the strength of feeling associated with them. It can be seen why detailed information is needed in order to combat these myths and to adjust the strategies to any unintended consequences of reform.

Changes in child care

Table 7.1 shows that the number of children in care or on supervision in the agency halved in three years. In fact if children living with parents, relatives or friends, placed with prospective adopters, or living independently are excluded the fall was over 70 per cent. The reduction in children placed in institutional care was 85 per cent whilst the numbers boarded out halved.

These census figures give an indication of the scale of changes that took place during the strategy. A more detailed study of changes in the circumstances and the numbers of children entering care has been published (Bilson and Thorpe 1988). This study focused on all the children entering care in April to September 1985 prior to the child care policy being implemented and those entering in the same six-month period in 1986. In the 1985 group, 124 children entered care compared with 78 in 1986. Neither this 37 per cent decrease in children entering care nor the overall reduction in children in care are explained by demographic changes. The

Table 7.1 Placements of children in care or under supervision 31.3.85 to 30.6.88

	31.3.85	30.6.86	30.6.87	30.6.88	decrease (%)
Home, relatives or friends (includes adopters and lodgings)	220	214	197	173	21
Boarded out	155	133	113	75	52
Residential homes	188	83	44	29	85
Other	10	4	2	1	90
Total	573	434	356	278	51

number of children in care or on supervision had fallen from close to the Scottish national average (per thousand 0–16-year-olds) to below half the average.

The study of children entering care before and after the policy changes showed that the decreases in entry to care were not uniform. In fact, those being removed from home due to ill-treatment, sexual abuse or neglect increased numerically (from 14 to 20 children) and formed over a quarter of the group in 1986. In addition to fewer children entering care in the 1986 period, these children spent less time away from home. The proportion remaining in statutory care a year after entry was just under a third in both groups.

These changes in the child care services had wider implications. Whilst there was a substantial increase in staff in the department (to the extent that there was an overall staff increase in 1986 compared with 1985), much of which was due to the transfer of funds from residential homes, not all of this was needed to provide services to children. There were thus increases in the resources available to provide services to other client groups. The changes in one part of the social work system had implications in other areas of service.

Whilst the changes in services to children were substantial, the survey of children entering care mentioned earlier raised two major areas of further concern. These related to children entering care due to ill treatment or neglect – an area of increase in entries – and to the problems of children who enter care due to their troublesome behaviour who were found to be unlikely to leave care until reaching school leaving age. Further work was undertaken in both these areas with further research combined with new resources and services. The identification of patterns thus made it possible to create adaptive strategies.

Case study 3

The third example of a systems approach concerns the management of the home help service by a local authority (Ross 1996). This example is, at the time of writing this, currently being undertaken by one of the writers and shows the way that a systems approach often develops in unanticipated directions. A review of the home help service was being undertaken to examine whether it required changes in order to demonstrate that it represented 'best value' for the council. Central to this was the need to find a way for users of the service to define what they valued about it. The views of service users provide an important source of information which can be compared with the views of managers to provide a form a 'double description' of the nature of the service. The review took place at a time when neighbouring authorities were contracting out their services causing redundancies and reduced pay and service conditions. In addition, both within the authority as elsewhere there was an increased focus on more specific contracts and tighter service standards. As home helps felt under threat it was important to demonstrate that the review was fair, showing its importance to the council and the need to develop rather than merely criticise.

Getting the views of home help service users is not easy. Response rates to questionnaires are frequently very low whilst interviews are time consuming and costly, often only covering a limited number of people. In order to raise morale whilst collecting important information on what service users valued an innovative method of collecting information was used. A competition for the 'Home Help of the Year' was designed where service users or their carers could nominate their home help for an award. In nominating the home help they had to state in no more than 50 words why their home help deserved to win by saying what it was about what they did which was important.

The competition was designed to show the value placed by the council on the home help service. Nominations was analysed to find what service users valued about the service they received. Fifty-three were nominated, this being more than one in six of all home helps. Analysis of the statements allowed patterns to be created. Four categories of nomination were found.

1. GOING THE EXTRA MILE

Many service users stressed the personal commitment of the home help as shown particularly by the home help doing more than the formally agreed services, often on a personal basis. Example statements included:

> When she heard my aunt was very ill she kept me company for a full day in the hospital room and visited her when she was sick. She shared her family Christmas meal with her.
>
> If I need something urgent out of hours all I need is to call her at home.
>
> She will shop for me in her own time and does my laundry.

2. PERSONAL CHARACTERISTICS

The greatest proportion of user feedback praised home helps in ways which did not relate to the tasks home helps actually performed but how much they were valued as people. Examples included:

> All times uncomplaining and very cheerful, she seems to really enjoy what she does. Brings a lot of cheer into painful days. It is a pleasure to have her come to my home.
>
> She talks to me as a person and not as an old aged pensioner.
>
> Carol has become a friend, not just my home help.
>
> She is always cheerful and vibrant within my home.
>
> She is my contact with the outside world and is good company.
>
> Ann has that extra something which is very special. It's like being part of her family with all her care and help. The day lights up when she calls 'Good morning'.
>
> The fact that my memory isn't as good as it was is no problem as her mind is so sharp. I look forward to seeing her as a friend and not just as a home help.
>
> I am recently disabled. I have never had to rely on anyone's help before and now find myself totally reliant on others. She has made it easier for me to accept help.

3. PERFORMANCE OF TASKS

Despite the large concentration of comments such as these above being on the character or behaviour of the home help, some comments did refer to the actual performance of tasks (what can be termed as outcomes). The following comments are examples of these:

> She is always on time.
>
> She puts me to bed every night.
>
> Very helpful in reading my correspondence and delivering my letters as my sight is not good.
>
> If I need a prescription, to call the doctor, or if I have a fall and hurt myself or if I have an asthma attack, she helps. She will also shop for me.

These comments were almost all reinforced by comments about the home help's personality – 'really friendly personality'; 'a cheery smile and a laugh'; 'so reliable and a winner to me', and so forth. This again seems to indicate that the beliefs the client has about the character, personality and motivation of the home help seem to be crucial in their appreciation of the volume and the nature of tasks the home help performs.

4. SUPPORT TO CARERS

As well as the above comments from users there were also nominations from carers and family members. These very clearly followed the patterns identified above. They particularly valued the personal characteristics of the home help, their capacity to 'go the extra mile' and their personal commitment and care to their relatives. Examples include:

> Maureen has been with my mother (94 years) for about three years. Mum can be trying at times but Maureen has never complained or let her down. She is very cheery and is very well liked by our family.
>
> My family think she is a lady and I second that.
>
> Working full-time it is not possible for me to visit my mum as I would want but knowing Laura is there gives me peace of mind.
>
> Helen is unfailingly sunny, helpful and kind to my elderly friend.
>
> She takes home washing, washes and cuts mum's hair, cuts her nails and cleans her clothes every day.
>
> I live a very lonely life as my husband has Alzheimer's so I look forward to her visits.

News of difference

These quotations from the nomination forms speak volumes about the aspects of the service people valued and what they believed to be important about their home help. In that sense they showed very clearly their beliefs about the service they receive which seems to be shared in many cases with that of their family members, carers and friends. The managerial imperatives surrounding the home help service at this time included greater contract specification, regularisation of home help hours and conditions of service, measurable outcomes for the service, performance indicators, 'best value' and formal standard setting. In short, as in many areas of public sector provision the move was to 'McDonaldise' it and bring it under rational control. Yet it was clear from the statements in the nominations that these standardisation measures were in sharp contrast to the valued aspects of the service. Trying excessively to proceduralise and rationalise in this way would thus be folly if it only leads to the loss of the valued elements of the service

This news of difference was of vital importance for the review. It fundamentally challenged the direction being taken in the management of the service. The issues about this direction of the service, however, went much wider than the managers within the department. The policy and practice in community care was increasingly coming under scrutiny from central government; from councillors rightly interested in ensuring that the budgets they allocated were well used and, through media publicity, public opinion of the services. It was important to address these wider systems if the valued elements of the home help system were to be protected.

The fact that the information was collected through a competition has proved helpful in the attempts to address these issues. The competition has provided the opportunity to publicise to the general public, local businesses providing partnership and prizes, to elected members who allocated resources to it and through the media who covered the 'Home Help of the Year' award, what the service was 'really' about. In particular, the local authority was able to promote through the users' own views of the service that it was not just about cleaning, shopping, cooking and monitoring vulnerable people at home, but was a highly valued service based on personal relationships and care.

At the same time within the department the information is being used to consider new approaches to the way home helps are recruited and trained and the way the service is to be developed (i.e. by encouraging and allowing flexibility in home help tasks rather than encouraging adherence to strict care plans and regularising tasks).

This example shows the way that in using a systems approach we are not outside the ecology for which we plan. The news of difference provided by the survey challenged the beliefs not only of other managers and those outside the service but also of the managers who set up the competition. The need to be open to adopting new and different understandings of the work is one of the challenges and the joy of a systems approach.

Summary

These case studies demonstrate the principles outlined for managerial and organisational change in the last chapter. At their heart is information which challenged and changed the epistemology of key participants. They show how the identification of patterns lead to adaptive strategies being introduced and the outcomes of changes being identified. The case studies provide examples of the tensions and creative opportunities which are generated when systems change and adapt.

Whilst organisational change in social work is no simple matter, it is necessary if services are to be improved in what is often a hostile environment for social work. The systems principles offer a framework which can be used to understand how change and stability in organisations is possible and this certainly offers more hope of positive outcomes than some social work research would suggest is generally happening.

CHAPTER 8

A Systems Approach to Social Work Education

I believe that the students were right in the sixties: there was something very wrong in their education and indeed in almost the whole culture. But I believe that they were wrong in the diagnosis of where the trouble lay. They fought for 'representation' and 'power'. On the whole they won their battles and now we have student representation. But it becomes increasingly clear that the winning of these battles for 'power' has made no difference to the educational process. The obsolescence to which I referred is unchanged and, no doubt, in a few years we shall see the same battles, fought over the same phoney issues, all over again.

Bateson, *Mind and Nature (1978)*

We tell ourselves that we are choosing our philosophy by scientific and logical criteria, but in truth our preferences are determined by the need to change from one posture of discomfort to another. Each theoretical system is a cop-out, tempting us to escape from the opposite fallacy.

Bateson and Bateson, *Angels Fear (1987)*

The persuasive power of empirical arguments in Western culture means that the use of data from information systems is likely to have a major impact on the organisations which use them ... the issue for professionals in organisations is no longer one of whether such systems provide an objective model of the operation of the services but instead the morality of the actions that they support. In this sense the information system moves from the peripheral position of a bureaucratic impediment to the 'real work' of the professional to centre stage as a key element in the social construction of the service.

Bilson, *Facts, Figures and Fantasy (1995)*

This chapter provides an overview of Bateson's theory of learning and its implications for training in social work illustrated by an example of the use of this approach to inform the curriculum, design and teaching of information technology (IT) on two social work qualifying courses. The development of these courses by one of the writers is chronicled more fully elsewhere (Bilson 1993, 1995).

Bateson's theory provides a framework for understanding the process of learning which is applicable to a range of different educational tasks. The current approach to social work education in the United Kingdom is essentially reductionist, focusing on breaking down social work practice into definable competencies. This competencies approach has become so universally accepted that to suggest that it is not appropriate to social work education seems almost heretical. However, an essential part of becoming a social worker is the adoption of values, and principles which underpin those values. Changing values requires learning which is of a different order to that required to gain a new skill or competency. In skills training new ways of responding to situations are learned and practised whilst the adoption, for example, of anti-discriminatory values requires changes not only in responses to situations but fundamentally in the way that situations are perceived. The recognised need that issues concerning values should permeate all teaching is itself problematic in a competencies approach but changing values requires learning of an entirely different type or level to that required to gain skills or competencies. Competence in social work is defined for the purposes of qualifying training in CCETSW's paper 30. The competency approach relies on the assessment of outcomes of training which starts with a statement of competence (FEU 1984): 'The possession and development of sufficient skills, knowledge, appropriate attitudes and experience for successful performance.' Overall competence is broken down into competencies which can include cognitive, attitudinal or psychomotor capabilities (FEU 1987) and the gaining and assessment of these competencies forms the basis of social work qualification and of post-qualification awards (CCETSW 1992). The reductionist nature of this approach and the way in which it appears to introduce a scientific approach to education have been attacked. For example, McLeish suggested it could be denounced as 'a form of scientism, the desire to make all educational values approximate to a tight system of measurement' and also because it does not include 'a recognition of the value of inner, subjective states' (1990). Within the social work profession Jordan offered a criticism of CCETSW's approach based on the conflicting value positions that the paper promotes – a radical agenda of anti-oppression alongside liberal values of respecting 'rights, privacy, confidentiality, choice' (1991). Similarly Harris (1985) suggested that social work training needed to promote creativity: 'social work practice depends less on the regurgitation of expertise learned by rote than on creative and often ingenious approaches to problem solving being applied to hitherto intractable problems.' Such creativity does not exist however in the statement of competencies. It is in the spirit of these criticisms of a competency approach that social work educators should consider basic issues about the nature of learning itself if a blinkered approach is to be avoided.

Bateson's theory of learning provides a basis for rethinking the approach to learning in the social work field. His paper 'The logical categories of learning and communication' (1973) attacks behaviourist models of learning which he suggests do not distinguish between items of behaviour – picking something from a shop's shelves – and ways an individual can organise patterns of behaviour – stealing from shops. To deal with this fundamental flaw in 'learning theory' he suggests a model for learning in which there is a hierarchy of levels of learning which he calls zero learning, learning I, learning II and learning III.

Like many commonly used terms the meaning of learning, although easily understood, can be difficult to define. Learning clearly represents some kind of change in an individual but to define what kind of change is, in Bateson's words, 'a delicate matter' (1993). In his definitions of the different levels of learning, Bateson specifies what sort of change is being discussed at each level.

Zero learning is where nothing new is learned. That is where behaviour is predetermined by, for example, genetics or by previous completed learning, such that every time the situation is encountered the response of the individual will be the same. One example of this is Pavlov's dogs after they had been trained. At this stage they would salivate every time they heard the signal. The dogs learned nothing from the signal and their response was unchanging.

Levels of learning beyond zero learning involve some degree of learning by trial and error. Learning I refers to the situation in which the individual chooses to respond to a stimulus from within a set of behavioural alternatives. Thus the original training of Pavlov's dogs is an example of learning of this level. In humans an example of this is what psychologists have termed rote learning. Many of the competencies defined in CCETSW paper 30 could be classified as being at the level of learning I.

Learning II is classified as learning to learn. As an example of this Bateson quotes Hull's experiments with people doing rote learning in which they had to learn to repeat sequences of syllables. Hull noticed that subjects involved in these experiments improved their ability to rote learn over a sequence of tests. Bateson points out that this change in the subject's ability to rote learn is not drawn from the particular set of syllables as these cannot provide information on the next set of syllables. Instead what is learnt relates to the subject's adaptation to the context of the rote learning. In other words, what has been learnt relates to the subject's understanding of the nature of the learning situation itself.

Learning II concerns transferability of learning which requires the subject to recognise that the context is one in which certain categories of responses are applicable. For example, a social worker who has the ability to use a number of counselling approaches needs the ability to assess the particular situation they face and to judge what approach will be the best to apply. Such an ability can be learned through what Bateson refers to as 'calibration' – repeated practice in situations which themselves are essentially unique. Similarly Harris suggests the transfer of learning requires 'a sensitive yet intellectually discriminating analysis of differences as well as similarities between situations' (1985).

Learning II is crucial to social work education. When a social worker encounters a problem his/her ability to solve it depends on recognising what sort of problem-solving behaviour is relevant to its solution. If the categorisation of the situation is incorrect the problem-solving behaviour may worsen the problem and lead a vicious spiral referred to as a 'more of the same' loop. An example of this is the situation in which a social worker attempts to reassure a seriously worried person. The response to reassurance is often to feel that the situation has not properly understood the reasons for worrying and to focus on these. Since the person now appears more worried more reassurance is given and a 'more of the same' loop is entered. Such a response is so common that many writers in the field of communication skills have classified reassurance as a block to communication (Bolton 1979). A key issue here being that the social worker's faulty learning II is not corrected by the failure of the worried person to 'learn' that they should not be so worried.

Learning III is concerned with changes in the sets of beliefs and assumptions which are used to make sense of experience (a person's epistemology). Previous chapters have discussed the importance of considering and changing these assumptions. This is a particularly important aspect of social work education and covers changing habitual practices through to considering issues of discrimination such as racism. Thus social work requires learning at all three of Bateson's levels.

The idea that there are different types of learning in higher education has been identified before. For example, research in higher education has identified two styles or approaches to learning which have been termed 'deep' and 'shallow' learning (Gibbs 1990). In terms of Bateson's model of learning these would be analogous to learning I and II. The choice of a deep or shallow approach would be based on the student's categorisation of the nature of the current situation and this would account for the fact that some students take a deep approach in one subject and not in another.

The competencies approach is effectively reductionist and relies on breaking down 'good' practice into a set of decontextualised skills, behaviours and pieces of knowledge. A corollary of this is that these competencies can then be taught in a 'modular' way and that once sufficient of them have been mastered the student will be capable of 'good' social work practice. The benefits of such an approach can be seen in the ability to specify what should be learnt, in assessing that learning and in being able to assess courses by measuring the extent to which students have achieved these competencies. This approach has serious flaws as a model for the training of social workers. First, the assumption that there is some single relatively stable body of knowledge, skills and behaviours which can be broken down in the first place is flawed. A second difficulty is that simply gaining the competencies is far from a guarantee that the student will be able to carry out good and sensitive social work practice in a range of contexts with a variety of individuals, families or other groups who need help. The issue here is exactly that which Bateson set out to address in his paper on learning. Social work is not simply a set of competencies but a way of organising responses to or understanding contexts in which social workers meet people in trouble. Whilst there are competencies – behaviours, knowledge, skills – which need to be learned (learning I) there is also the crucial issue of how to integrate or understand this learning so that when a new situation is encountered the social worker will engage helpfully rather than unhelpfully. Learning II of this type requires that the student has the opportunity to calibrate their use of social work approaches in a variety of contexts. Finally this transferable learning requires an epistemological framework appropriate to the tasks of social work. Student social workers will need help to examine the beliefs and values that shape their actions. Key issues such as the ethical framework for their actions need to be considered so that action does not take place in a moral vacuum. Similarly they will need to reflect on and possibly change their assumptions about such issues as the possibility of change in individuals, groups and communities.

Implications of the approach for training in social work

The implications for a model for learning social work are wide. Previous chapters have dealt with the issue of how to change epistemologies. From these discussions it will be seen that such change is not likely to be achieved through a logical argument or the use of power to assert 'what is right and true'. As always Bateson's writing gives a framework within which a range of approaches to learning (and hence to teaching) can be developed but it does not specify a particular approach. The focus of education within this framework is not on decontextualised competencies but on the overall learning experience.

The idea that there are differences between levels of learning is useful to curriculum planning as well as to planning the teaching of individual sessions. It allows the trainer to consider what the key areas are for those participating in the particular training session(s). The writers' commitment to the need for a clear epistemological basis for social work practice will be clear to readers. Attempting to teach techniques or skills without being explicit about their basis would not only be impractical but unethical. This is not to say that trainees need to adopt the epistemology being proposed, but rather that they should not be presented with skills, techniques or theoretical perspectives without considering the assumptions on which they are based. In this approach students are encouraged to compare their own assumptions with those of the teachers providing opportunities for news of difference. This is similar to Keeney and Ross's (1985) suggestions for family therapy training and the systems approach to research proposed by Atkinson and Heath who state (1987):

> the process we are suggesting is one in which the researchers retrace the distinctions they have drawn in constructing any view of the data, so that

> the reader may do likewise. In a sense, the reader is taught the process of constructing a view. Once readers learn the particular way of drawing distinctions proposed and illustrated by a researcher, they can begin applying the set of distinctions in their own daily experiences. Readers will decide the legitimacy of the set of distinctions as they try it out for themselves.

The following example shows the practical implication of an attempt to apply this model to the introduction of a new subject – Introduction to Information Technology. The Introduction of the Information Technology teaching took place in a context which had major constraints. The students on the social work courses were in the main re-entrants to education, often with few or limited educational qualifications and many of them had little experience of computers. Additionally, the course focused on the use of client information systems which hit on a particular issue for many of these students in that it involved skills in numeracy. This was an area in which some of the students had bad experiences of prior learning, often feeling that they were 'blocked' and unable to carry out even simple computations. In addition, whilst information systems are increasingly used in social work agencies they are frequently seen as a tool of bureaucratic management to control and monitor services rather than being for direct use by practitioners. Steyaert (1992) suggests that this has become a self-fulfilling prophecy in social work with social workers seeing computers as a threat to their professional values. This is despite the fact that the importance of knowledge of computer systems is increasingly needed by social workers for a whole variety of reasons. For example, with the increasing use of the Internet by paedophile groups it is important for child protection work to include vigilance on such matters. One of the writers has produced guidance for social workers on this area (Bilson 1998) as well as a resource database on the Internet.[1] It is our belief that social workers increasingly need skills in understanding new technology to gain from its many benefits such as access to a vast range of information[2] and the ability quickly to exchange ideas and experiences through discussion forums as well as to guard against its misuse.

1 The resource database and the advice to social workers on child safety is available on the Centre for Europe's Children's web site http://Eurochild.gla.ac.uk

2 For example the Centre for Europe's Children's web site (see footnote 1) and the Asia Europe Meeting's Child welfare resource database (http://ASEM.gla.ac.uk), which are both managed by one of the writers, provide a massive range of information on children's rights and the commercial sexual exploitation of children freely available to social workers through the world wide web.

A key issue suggested by the model was that it would be important to concentrate on learning II and learning III rather than learning I. Although some basic skills in use of keyboards would have to be learnt. Earlier chapters have discussed the McDonaldisation of social work and there was an ever-present danger that unless a different epistemological framework was offered, teaching which focused on information systems would perpetuate this. In addition, a key part of all the teaching on the course was anti-oppressive practice which meant that the teaching would need to encourage students to consider the way their values affected their practice – for example, information systems on child protection might provide evidence of institutional racism or sexism and help students to confront their own attitudes and beliefs about oppressive practices.

Learning II would be particularly important because it was unlikely that particular software or computers would be used in the agencies in which the students were to work, but skills in understanding principles of data management would be useful whatever the equipment.

The key issue in adopting the approach with respect to the overall programme was to provide students with a learning situation which would encourage learning at the appropriate level and in view of the nature of the course this would require attention to levels I, II and III.

The focus of the course was the use of information rather than on the use of information technology. This was aimed at encouraging students to learn basic skills in using computers, but the main concentration was on developing an understanding of the nature and use of information in improving services for social work clients. The framework used for this was the systems one put forward in this book. Thus information was viewed as relational and not objective. To encourage learning II it would be necessary to help students to develop the ability to learn how to approach the use of information in a variety of contexts and to motivate them to do so by helping them to become aware of the benefits of such an approach (Bilson 1995):

> The starting point ... is a focus on the use of information rather than on the technology. As the aim is to empower professionals to use information, developing skills in interpreting and presenting information are equally, if not more important than technical skills with databases. The participants are therefore involved in projects which simulate the use of information to bring about improvements in services. The main focus is on developing an understanding of the nature and use of information; its effects on services for social work clients and on designing strategies to

improve services. Thus the approach focuses on areas which are central to social work – strategies for change.

The programme started by providing Bateson's definition of information and suggesting this as the framework. It was shown how different patterns could be discerned in the same data and how the visibility of these patterns depended on the assumptions of the person analysing the data.

It is important in a systems approach to understand the student's perception of the nature of the learning situation. Possible blocks to learning have been identified earlier and they included the perceived relevance of the subject, the practical nature of students' expectations about the course, and general beliefs in social work about information technology. To minimise these problems the programme was built around using actual client information systems to illustrate particular points about database systems in relation to their structure, usage and application rather than taking the commonly used approach of giving a theoretical overview and moving from this to its specific application. Throughout the course a key issue was that of language and the need to give these students access to the terminology and current issues in information technology without confusing them with an overload of new terms and concepts in an attempt to demystify and empower the students. The aims of the course are shown below (Bilson 1995).

(a) Introduction to common terms and vocabulary

A common problem for newcomers to information technology is the abundance of technical terms and jargon. Many social workers are disempowered by what appears to be a foreign language. If they can be helped to gain an understanding of the vocabulary of new technology then this alone might help to allay fears and enable them to participate in critical debates about the uses made of computers in the organisations in which they practice.

(b) Introduction to a constructivist[3] approach to the use of information

This is a key aspect of the approach. The idea is to help participants to gain a critical understanding of information systems and their

3 The constructivist position mentioned here was developed by Bilson (1997) and is similar to Bateson's view about the lack of objective experience. It is assumed that observers participate in the construction of the reality that they experience. This moves from the traditional view of information as representation of an external reality. The implication of this is that information systems do not provide a model of an independently existing external reality; instead the actions of those who use them bring forth a reality that is mutually specified by their interactions with the system (extraction of data etc.) and the pre-understandings (epistemology) that the users bring to it.

implications for the organisations in which they are used. The constructivist approach focuses on the use of information as a key element in the social construction of the workplace. Rather than simply provide a critique of uses of information systems, the aim is to ensure participants have the skills and knowledge both to critically analyse the use of information systems and to use them as a powerful tool in the construction of services which empower service users.

(c) Consider the ethics of the use of client information systems

In rejecting representationalism the constructivist approach brings to the foreground the ethics of any particular use of information systems. A key focus of the approach is to consider the ways in which information systems can be used in strategies to combat oppression as well as to ensure that their use is not oppressive.

The course provided a number of opportunities for students to work in the computer laboratories, but more importantly it focused on work in small groups using actual information systems with real data (with names and other identifying factors removed). For example, one group of students was given a database containing anonymised details of the child protection registrations in a local authority. Differences in practice with regard to the registration of sexual abuse cases were apparent in the data and their simulated task was to make a presentation to one of the teams which had never registered a child for sexual abuse. Their task was thus not only to extract information from the computer, but also to consider its meaning and its use in changing social work practice.

This approach encouraged students to develop skills in understanding data and the exercises were designed to simulate the use of information systems in presentations to social work staff or consumers to help them to change the way services were delivered. It was within this context that students confronted numerical data and this was designed to be very different from that in which numeracy skills had been required previously. Students were encouraged particularly to consider the patterns of service which the data demonstrated. For example, this included the difference of provision with regard to sex and race. In this way stereotypical responses could be identified from the data and additionally their own assumptions about what they would find were used to challenge their ideas about, for example, the nature and extent of institutional sexism and racism. One of the anonymised databases contained information about the ethnic origin of a group of children who had been the subject of child protection investigations. Black children were over-represented in the data and there was considerable debate about why this was and how the institutional racism, that the student group doing the presentation felt was represented by the data, could best be challenged in the simulation of a presentation to a group of managers in the child protection agency. Another group using an anonymised database of court outcomes were asked to hypothesise about the gender differences that might be apparent from the data. When quite different patterns of recommendations in court reports and levels and types of outcomes were found to those they had thought would be there it occasioned some discussion of issues of gender and the complex nature of sexism. Thus the use of simulations gave the opportunity for students to compare and challenge beliefs and assumptions about issues of power, privilege and prejudice.

Over time and through learning from feedback given by students a number of features were developed in the teaching programme. A full account of the programme is given in Bilson (1995). Apart from the theoretical overview and some introductory sessions in the computer laboratories the teaching took place increasingly through small group work developing presentations as described above. Each group had an allocation of a consultant's time which they could use as they wanted, calling meetings as they required them and with control over the agenda. Thus the relationship with students moved to one of consultant and consultee rather than teacher and student. The group's simulated task of presenting information to a particular audience (for example as if they were attending a management meeting) was developed and became assessed through peer assessment. Students were thus involved in receiving and giving feedback on presentations. They also became involved in the process of evaluating presentations giving them another perspective on the learning situation.

Learning within this model is not confined to students and it is important to get feedback about responses to the teaching. Information about responses to the information technology teaching were sought by means of mid-way reviews, group meetings and the use of questionnaires. Comments were generally positive, for example 92 per cent of respondents agreed with the statement that the exercises were informative and interesting and 72 per cent said the use of computer laboratories were informative and interesting. One comment illustrated the issues mentioned above: 'This was a totally new area to me ... I was apprehensive at first. I feel quite confident about information technology now.' Students did find peer assessment difficult the first time it was used and the course was changed to give the opportunity to discuss assessment giving another opportunity to reflect upon the learning situation as a whole.

In this way the information technology teaching, instead of focusing on the use of software, became a forum in which students were encouraged to consider the nature of information, to think about how to change social work practice and challenge oppression, to reflect on their own patterns of practice, and even on the nature of their own learning situation. Interestingly, students often became motivated to use computers to present information through graphs and diagrams, gaining skills well beyond those initially envisaged. The following comment from one of the groups demonstrates the way that this approach helped them to think about teamwork (Bilson 1995):

> During the process of researching and preparing for this assignment, the group has not only learnt about the nature of data base information and its relevance to social work, but also about the group process. It became clear that working as a group was a crucial factor and because we felt it had been so important, we felt it would be useful to list the following areas we identified as significant elements:
>
> - The need for direction and organisation of the group, perhaps in the form of a chairperson
> - The importance of the appropriate allocation of tasks and the acknowledgement of individual skills and preferred methods of working
> - The utilisation of the various skills of each group member to their full advantage
> - The importance of effective communication skills and group consensus
> - The need for constant review and evaluation within the group.

These lessons were probably hard won as can be seen in the fact that they added 'Had we experienced these areas earlier the process may have been more effective.'

Conclusion

Bateson's theory of learning provides a powerful new framework for social work education which starts with the idea that there are different levels of learning. Using the theory within a systems approach directly addresses such important issues as the individual's epistemologies including values and other assumptions. It also gives a framework which encourages a focus on transferability of learning. In social work education these issues cannot be ignored as they are central to the endeavour.

This is in contrast to the current competencies approach to social work education which is ineffective because of its reductionist basis. This makes it unable to deal with the different types of learning necessary in social work. In particular it cannot help individuals synthesise the different competencies into the more coherent whole necessary to practice social work. It also risks encouraging the teaching of decontextualised skills and techniques drawn from different, and often incompatible, theoretical frameworks.

The example given above shows how Bateson's theory can be used to inform curricular planning and even the teaching of individual sessions. It encourages the development of a learning context focused on the individual as a whole as well as the particular nature of what is to be taught. The theory provides a framework within which systems ideas such as information as 'news of difference' can be used to provide powerful and innovative learning experiences.

CHAPTER 9

The Development of Systems Ideas in Social Work for the Future

'So Successful and their Beliefs are so Heartless'

> I think cybernetics is the biggest bite out of the Fruit of the Tree of Knowledge that mankind has taken over the last two thousand years. But most of the bites of the apple have proved to be rather indigestible – usually for cybernetic reasons.
>
> Bateson, *Steps to an Ecology of Mind (1972)*

> I am appalled by my scientific colleagues, and while I disbelieve almost everything that is believed by the counter-culture, I find it more comfortable to live with that disbelief than with the dehumanising disgust and horror that conventional occidental themes and ways of life inspire in me. They are so successful and their beliefs are so heartless.
>
> Bateson, *Angels Fear (1988)*

Bateson's work, and that of his distinguished research colleagues, transformed the practice of psychotherapy not by laying down a series of psychotherapeutic techniques, but by redefining the nature of therapy itself. The proposition made in this book is that Batesonian ideas, applied to the theory, management and practice of social work, will inform social work not by producing blueprints for practice or methodologies for intervention, but by suggesting a new analysis of social work based on an ecology of practice underpinned by systems principles.

In his 1958 epilogue to his book *Naven* Bateson tells a story about the philosopher Whitehead. Whitehead's former pupil and famous collaborator Bertrand Russell came to Harvard University to lecture on quantum theory, which was not only new but difficult to understand. Russell tried to make his subject intelligible to the distinguished audience who were unfamiliar with mathematical ideas. When he sat down Whitehead congratulated him on his brilliant speech, 'especially on leaving unobscured ... the vast darkness of the subject'. Bateson defines all science as an attempt (1958):

> to cover with explanatory devices – and thereby to obscure – the vast darkness of the subject. It is a game in which the scientist uses his explanatory principles according to certain rules to see if these principles can be stretched to cover the vast darkness.

He adds that the game has a deeper purpose which is to learn something about the nature of explanation – the process of 'knowing'. Hence Bateson's constant concern with epistemology and the nature of knowledge. When looking at the future of systems theories in social work it must be said that systems ideas leave the vast darkness of human behaviour and interaction relatively unobscured. They do not explain why things happen or provide blueprints of action, nor can they provide ultimate 'truths', because none of these lie within the framework of systems theory. Yet despite this we believe that systems ideas are relevant and useful in the pragmatic world of social work and the management of social services.

This new edition of *Social Work Management and Practice* comes ten years after its original publication. This period has seen major changes in social work and in its image within society. In the original book we made optimistic predictions about future developments in the application of systems ideas. We were predicting a continuation of the rapid inroads of systems ideas into social work practice and management. Unfortunately our optimism has proved largely unfounded and few of the things we predicted have come into fruition. We were, however, more successful in our analysis of the difficulties that would be faced in applying Bateson's ideas as follows:

> There are many difficulties with the application of Bateson's ideas in social work, because of its own culture and ethos. Its belief system is still largely based on intrapsychic phenomena, its values are broadly anti-intellectual and practical and its theoretical constructs are, at best, based on an eclectic cocktail of very divergent theories of human nature and at worst little better than 'if it feels right do it'. Similarly, social work in Thatcherite Britain which is practised in the often hostile political arena of Local Authority politics, is not always the best environment for new ideas to be introduced and for old certainties to be challenged. Social work has many enemies and, for some, this systemic framework

may appear to be another uncaring onslaught which provides ultimately fewer certainties for practitioners.

The ten years since the first edition have seen developments in social work which must be the context for our comments in this chapter. In looking at this period we are giving our own view of developments coloured by our personal histories and experiences in social work practice, management and education and it does not represent a researched history of the period.

Within the United Kingdom we have seen a continuing worsening of the image of social work. Alongside the inquiries and scandals surrounding child deaths there has been an increase in cases in which workers in residential homes, day care and in nurseries have seriously abused children, elderly people and other vulnerable service users. These cases have been widely publicised with good reason. The media's focus on this small proportion of bad practice far outweighs the many examples of good work which receive no publicity. The social work journal *Community Care* (10–16 December 1998) said 'to suggest that some newspapers' coverage of social work lacks balance, measure and fairness risks winning an award for understatement of the year'. The introduction of the policy of care in the community has similarly brought a degree of bad press as people with a mental illness are increasingly seen living rough on the streets or in exceptional cases committing assaults or even murder. Inevitably the media's focus is on what it characterises as this failure of social work and there is no recognition of the vast number of people who have gained new lives and independence rather than continuing institutional care. The profession has also been criticised for being too 'politically correct' (see for example *Community Care* 23 December 1997) with cases of opposition to inter-racial adoption, or adoption by gay or lesbian couples providing the ammunition for this with little defence given. The images of social workers swing widely from dangerous – 'like the SAS in cardies and Hush Puppies' (*Sunday People* 28 September 1997, cited in Franklin 1998) – to bumbling bureaucrats; stereotypes of social workers as 'too soft, ineffectual, inexperienced incompetent, lack common sense and fail to protect children', working for agencies which lack subtlety and sensitivity to the rights of clients. One of the worse descriptions of this was Norman Tebbit's when he referred to 'the great blunderbuss (and blunder is usually the right word) of the Social Services' (Tebbit 1997). If it were true that there is no such thing as bad publicity our profession would be indeed very well placed in today's society. Yet as one of the writers (Ross 1999b) has argued elsewhere, the profession's bad publicity is now a critical matter for social work since its poor image deters people from coming for services they need. It also undermines the profession's case for resources (Ross 1999b):

> With probably the most media conscious Government ever in power ... resource and management decisions about the future of our services are being taken to assuage public opinion, whether we like it or not. In such a climate 'not to give a damn' about bad publicity is a high risk strategy which is likely to fail.

Whilst it is tempting to blame the media wholly for the poor image of social work it is the writers' view that the image is at least in part due to social workers' and social work managers' actions in the public arena and in particular the limited and often contradictory beliefs, assumptions and practices upon which social work actions are based. As Evans and Kearney (1996) say:

> a negative spiral has developed, where the poor public image, combined with lack of resources and more demands, has made workers and agencies defensive with the result that there is concentration on the negative aspects of work with service users and more positive aspects are ignored.

As a response to many of the scandals and inquiries in social work there have been a range of attempts to bring the actions of social workers and their managers under rational control. The new legal frameworks being implemented have increasingly been accompanied by prescriptive and controlling procedures which attempt to legislate for good practice. These measures have included procedures, guidance notes, 'memoranda' of practice, national standards and other mechanisms to regulate and proceduralise a profession which is based on caring and the uniqueness of human interaction. In Chapter 8 we provide a critique of the changes in social work education which have increasingly been based on the reductionist concept of competencies with its idea that good practice can be broken down into smaller components (skills, behaviours, knowledge) and that these can then be taught and assessed. We firmly believe that rational approaches which involve decontextualising practice and splitting down social work into individual behaviours, actions and competencies and removing these from the emotions and feelings which occur between 'helper' and those receiving help are doomed to fail. They take the rationality of the 'head' in the work but take away the 'head' and the 'heart' acting in harmony.

Inside social work we have seen a number of changes. The introduction of community care has brought the concept of 'care packages' and the new role of care management which focuses on the coordination and financial management of sets of services with little or no space for direct provision by social workers. This approach is increasingly being used in other areas of practice with traditional social work roles being superseded by the management of practical support or, in the case of child protection and work with offenders, community surveillance. In Chapter 6 we have provided our criticism of the new managerialism that is based on an increasingly rational approach which at its worse knows the cost of everything and the value of nothing. We fundamentally reject the view that the work social workers do can be broken down into purchasing and commissioning schedules which can be sealed in contracts and evaluated by methods based on accountancy.

On a more positive note the decade has seen a greater concentration within the profession on practice and services which stem from an ethical and moral framework particularly in relation to anti-oppressive and anti-discriminatory practice. The recognition of the discriminatory and oppressive forms of work which many service users suffered from such as people with disabilities, black and ethnic minority service users, women and gays and lesbians has sensitised workers and their agencies to important issues of discrimination. However, we have also seen times when those promoting these ideas have acted in oppressive ways to friends and colleagues who have dared to challenge the orthodoxy or who have been slow to adopt the 'correct' terms or way of thinking. It is our view that if oppression is to be attacked it must be challenged in all its forms, including the oppression that comes from the belief that there is a 'correct' way to be or to think. It is important that we try to remain open to what Bill Jordan (Jordan and Brandon 1979) has called acting in 'bad faith'. This applies as much to our own certainties as to the actions of others. Hence the reason why this edition of the book carries a much heavier emphasis on ethics and the myth of power (Preston-Shoot 1990).

Out of the iron cage of rationality

The decade since the first edition of this book has seen a background of increasing external and internal pressures to bring the actions of social work under rational control. Like Weber, Bateson saw society becoming increasingly trapped within an 'iron cage of rationality'. He saw an increasing split in which extremes of superstition were seen as the only alternative to the rationality of the occidental scientific approach. The theme of all Bateson's work is that these extremes are both due to errors in our basic epistemology which remains linear. Within social work the rise of new managerialism, with its reductionist and quantitative emphasis on performance indicators, best value, monitoring, and ever-more prescriptive procedures has not stemmed the flow of tragedies, protected people better or provided better services. It is this sort of applications of 'rationality' which Bateson, in the quotation at the head of this chapter, stated were so successful and yet so heartless. In trying to find inspiration in Bateson's ideas this book has tried to show that it is possible to have an approach which is both thinking and feeling. The systems framework provides a basis for this. Its rejection of simple linear rationality does not suggest that anything goes so long as it feels right. The chapters on practice and management in this book show how the difficult theoretical ideas provide principles which can guide sensitive and innovative practice. They show that information, monitoring and research can have a major part in informing social work management and practice in contrast to their overly concrete and controlling use in current approaches. The practice examples have demonstrated that a systems framework values individual professional autonomy rather than limiting it and can stimulate innovation rather than the dreary sameness, routine procedures and conformity that so often results from the increasingly McDonaldised services with which we have become so familiar.

We believe they show too that social work can bring positive creative changes in lives of individuals and to organisations and groups if it is practised in a thoughtful and sensitive way using both the intellect and emotions and feelings – the head and the heart together. To work in this way is a privilege and a challenge.

Whether these ideas will gain any major influence on social work is a matter of speculation. Like Bateson, we see extreme danger in the increased rational control being applied to the social work profession and fear its irrational outcomes. In his invitation to a conference addressing the pathology of occidental scientific premises Bateson asks the question, 'If we adopt a false epistemology, will we create, quickly or slowly, those circumstances which by their horror disprove our premises?' (1976). It will be sad if the only way that systems approaches gain any prominence is when the horror of the sorts of disasters which we have wrought on our environment are also wrought on our societies and communities.

The question that this book has proposed can be simply expressed as 'do systems ideas really matter to social workers?' Bateson believed that they provided the only way for mankind to survive. Without it, he believed the whole ecology was doomed. This book suggests that, without the integration of systems ideas into social work, only higher orders of pathology will be created by social work intervention. Social work responses to individuals and families have effects on and are determined by the larger ecosystem which is our society. In child protection the broad patterns of over-reaction and control have been identified in a whole range of research and the research of one of the writers shows how unrestrained social work intervention justified by scant theory has had devastating effects on many people's lives (Bilson and Thorpe 1998; Thorpe and Bilson 1998b). However, it is not just in child protection that the part social workers play in the ecology can be discerned. Social work has a major role in the definition and control of disadvantaged groups in society (for example those in poverty, older people, people with disabilities and mental illness, offenders, children etc.). The contention here is that the epistemology of social work does matter and that, despite all the difficulties, any examination of social work must address its part in the ecology of our society.

Social work must address the consequences of its actions, not by a greater concentration on the characteristics of the individuals it tries to help, but on the outcomes of its interventions with individuals, families and communities. Social workers have to address the epistemological basis for their interventions or they will continue to fail to be anything other than the scapegoats for society's ills. Despite the concern for the welfare of others which spawned the social work profession, it can and often does prove ultimately damaging to those it tries to help if the interventions do not respect the ecology of our clients' lives.

In view of all the difficulties, attempts to apply systems ideas to social work may still be stepping where angels fear to tread. It certainly requires that difficult questions are continually asked about the rationale for intervention and about the outcomes of intervention. Such an exercise is inevitably only a place to start. Undoubtedly, the adoption of systems ideas requires a major shift in our thinking about social work to occur. Such a shift confronts social workers with the results of their actions in a way which, for many, threatens chaos. It also offers the hope of an ecology of practice governed by, and continually responsive to, feedback about the results of social work intervention. Such an ecology of practice would offer real possibilities for helping clients within their social system and within their communities. We do not have to find that, in Thorpe's words, 'the enlightened Frankenstein of social work has created yet another monster'

(Thorpe *et al.* 1980). Social work can be an activity based on realism and on respect for the client's ecology. In order to do that it needs to escape from the iron cage of rationality and adopt an epistemology that encourages autonomy and innovation.

Our own views about the importance of social work escaping from the prison of McDonaldisation are clear from the text. This is not an esoteric view based on an ideological commitment to systems ideas, but one which has resonance with the views of those who matter most in social work – service users. The following examples provide the most eloquent call for social workers and their managers to find an approach which can encompass both the head and the heart:

> After I became totally disabled it was my social worker who helped me to accept help from other people.
>
> *Man aged 43 receiving community care services*

> My reason for writing is to express my appreciation for the care given. I have been ill for five years with several spells in hospital for surgery and every time I come home to my empty house it feels as if I have a family. Nothing which I need is ever regarded as too much trouble. Their supervisor gives a great lead to her team in being able to deal with everything without being patronising.
>
> *Woman aged 75 receiving community care services*

> I would like to take this opportunity to commend the professional attitude, care and dedication displayed by the social worker. He shared an ability to look into a situation and see what is really going on. He delved beyond the facade to see the truth. I appreciate very much the caring manner in which he approached the boys.
>
> *Mother of two children whose children were under the supervision of a social worker*

> I would ask that my son's social worker remain involved with him as he has built up such a trusting relationship with my son which has helped him overcome his problems.
>
> *Mother of a young person aged 16 years*

> Our first contact with social work was from the 'physical impairment service'. One was apprehensive of visits but this was quite unnecessary. The tenderness shown was wonderful.
>
> *Disabled man aged 70*

> It has given us a lot of strength and comfort during mum's illness to know she was surrounded by so many caring people … Our thanks for all you did for our mum. We'll not forget you.
>
> *Relatives of woman who died in residential care following a long illness*

These examples show what social work means to some of those for whom we provide and the positive impact on their lives. The systems approach outlined in this book provides a theoretical basis, guiding principles and real examples for practitioners and managers who wish to practice in ways which make real differences to the lives of those touched by social work. There can be no greater challenge to social work professionals than that of working with their heads and hearts to provide caring services for those who need them.

Bibliography

Adams, R., Allard, S., Baldwin, J. and Thomas, J. (1981) *Measure of Diversion.* Leicester: National Youth Bureau.

Adler, J. and Levy, C. (1981) 'The impact of the one-way screen: Its use as a teaching aid.' *Contemporary Social Work Education* 4, 65–74.

Anderson, T. (1992) 'Relationship, language and pre-understanding in the reflecting process'. *Australian and New Zealand Journal of Family Therapy 13,* 2, 87–91.

Anderson, T. (ed) (1991) *The Reflecting Team: Dialogues and Dialogues about the Dialogues.* New York: Norton.

Armstrong, J.S. (1982) 'Strategies for implementing change: An experiential approach.' *Group and Organization Studies* 7, 4, 457–75.

Atkinson, B.J. and Heath, A.W. (1990) 'Further thoughts on second-order family therapy – this time it's personal.' *Family Process* 29, 145–55.

Atkinson, B.J. and Heath, A.W. (1987) 'Beyond objectivism and relativism: Implications for family therapy research.' *Journal of Strategic and Systemic Therapies* 1, 8–17.

Auerswald, E.H. (1968) 'Interdisciplinary versus ecological approach.' *Family Process* 7, 202–12.

Bales, R.F., Hare, A.P. and Borgatta, E.C. (1955) *Small Groups.* New York: A.A. Knopf.

Bandler, R. and Grinder, J. (1982) *Reframing.* Utah: Real People Press.

Barker, R. and Bilson, A. (1998) *Children in State Care and Contact – the Experience of Northborough.* Newcastle: Manor House Publications.

Bartlett, H.M. (1970) *The Common Base of Social Work Practice.* New York: National Association of Social Workers.

Bateson, G. (1991) *A Sacred Unity: Further Steps to an Ecology of Mind.* New York: Harper Collins.

Bateson, G. (1981) 'A comment by Gregory Bateson.' In J. Haley, *Reflections on Therapy.* Washington, DC: Family Therapy Institute.

Bateson, G. (1980) *Mind and Nature – A Necessary Unity.* London: Fontana.

Bateson, G. (1977) 'Afterword.' In J. Brockman (ed), *About Bateson.* Toronto: Brockman Associates.

Bateson, G. (1976) 'Mind/body dualism conference: position papers'. *CoEvolution Quarterly,* Fall.

Bateson, G. (1973) *Steps to an Ecology of Mind.* New York: Paladin.

Bateson, G. (1958) *Naven,* 2nd edn with added epilogue.

Bateson, G. and Bateson, M.C. (1988) *Angels Fear: An Investigation into the Nature and the Meaning of the Sacred.* London: Rider.

Bateson, G. Jackson, D.D., Haley, J. and Weakland, J. (1963) 'A note on the double bind – 1962.' *Family Process* 2, 154–61.

Bateson, G. Jackson, D.D., Haley, J. and Weakland, J. (1956) 'Toward a theory of schizophrenia.' *Behavioural Science* 1, 251–64.

Beer, S. (1974) *Designing Freedom.* London: Wiley.

Biestek, F. (1957) *The Casework Relationship.* London: George Allen and Unwin.

Bilson, A. (1998) 'Child safety on the Internet: A child rights approach.' *Professional Social Work,* November (also available on the Internet at http://Eurochild.gla.ac.uk).

Bilson, A. (1997) 'Guidelines for a constructivist approach: Steps towards the adaptation of ideas from family therapy for use in organizations.' *Systems Practice* 10, 2, 153–78.

Bilson, A. (1996) 'Bringing forth organisational realities: A constructivist approach to the management of change in human services.' PhD thesis, Lancaster University, Lancaster.

Bilson, A. (1995) 'Facts, figures and fantasy: A constructivist approach to teaching information technology.' In B. Kolleck and J. Rafferty (eds) *Both Sides: Technology and Human Services,* Berlin: Alice-Salomon-Fachhochschule. (This was the first entirely electronically published book on human services and can be viewed on the Internet at http://www.soton.ac.uk/~chst/both/ both.htm).

Bilson, A. (1993) 'Applying Bateson's theory of learning to social work education.' *Social Work Education* 12, 1, 46–61.

Bilson, A. (1986) 'A counter-productive strategy.' *Community Care* 623, 16–17.

Bilson, A. (1985) 'Care and custody in Ogwr.' Research Report, NCH Wales, Cardiff.

Bilson, A. and Barker, R. (1998) 'Looked after children and contact: Reassessing the social work task.' *Research, Policy and Planning* 16, 1, 20–7.

Bilson, A. and Barker, R. (1995) 'Parental contact in foster care and residential care after the Children Act.' *British Journal of Social Work* 25, 3, 367–381.

Bilson, A. and Barker, R. 'Siblings of children in care or accommodation: A neglected area of practice.' *Practice* 6, 4, 226–35.

Bilson, A. and Ross, S. (1981) 'The Sunshine Group: An example of social work intervention through the use of a group.' *Groupwork* 4, 1, 15–28.

Bilson, A. and Thorpe, D.H. (1998) 'Refocussing child protection services.' *Professional Social Work* 12, 373–381.

Bilson, A. and Thorpe, D.H. (1988) *Managing Child Care Careers.* Glenrothes: Fife Regional Council Social Work Department.

Bolton, R. (1979) *People Skills.* New Jersey: Prentice Hall.

Booth, T. and Bilson, A. (1988) 'Fit enough for care.' *Nursing Times* 84, 29, 42–45.

Booth, T., Bilson, A. and Fowell, I. (1990) 'Staff attitudes and caring practices in homes for the elderly.' *British Journal of Social Work* 20, 117–131.

Borwick, I. (1986) 'The family therapist as business consultant.' In L.C. Wynne, S.H. McDaniel and T.T. Weber (eds) *Systems Consultation – A New Perspective for Family Therapy.* London: Guildford Press.

Brand, D. (1996) 'Power play.' *Community Care,* 31 October: 8.

Breslin, D.C. and Cade, B.W. (1981) 'Intervening in family systems using observer messages.' *Journal of Marital and Family Therapy* 7, 453–60.

Brockman, J. (1977) *About Bateson,* Toronto: Brockman Associates.

Cade, B.W. (1986) 'The reality of "reality" (or the "reality" of "reality"). *American Journal of Family Therapy* 14, 49–56.

Cade, B.W. (1982) 'Some uses of metaphor.' *Australian Journal of Family Therapy* 3, 3, 135–40.

Cade, B.W. and Cornwall, M. (1983) 'The evolution of the one-way screen.' *Australian Journal of Family Therapy* 4, 2, 73–80.

Campbell, D. and Draper, R. (eds) (1985) *Applications of Systemic Family Therapy: The Milan Approach.* London: Grune and Stratton.

Casteneda, C. (1972) *Journey to Ixtlan.* London: Penguin.

CCETSW (1992) *The Requirements for Post Qualifying Education and Training in the Personal Social Services.* Paper 31, London: CCETSW.

Cecchin, G. (1992) 'Constructing therapeutic possibilities.' In S. McNamee and K.J. Gergen (eds) *Therapy as Social Constitution.* London: Sage.

Cecchin, G. (1987) 'Hypothesizing, circularity, and neutrality revisited: An invitation to curiosity.' *Family Process* 26, 4, 405–13.

Checkland, P.B. (1972) 'Towards a system-based methodology for real-world problem-solving.' In G. Vickers (ed) *Systems Behaviour.* London: Harper and Row.

Clyde Report (1992) *Report of the Inquiry into the Removal of Children from Orkney in February 1991.* Edinburgh: HMSO.

Cohen, S. (1985) *Visions of Social Control.* Oxford: Basil Blackwell.

Dávilla, J. (1993) 'Foucault's interpretive analytics of power.' *Systems Practice* 6, 4, 383–405.

Dell, P. (1982) 'Beyond homeostasis'. *Family Process* 21, 21–41.

Dell, P.F. (1986) 'In defense of lineal causality.' *Family Process* 25, 513–21.

Derrida, J. (1978) *Writing and Difference.* Chicago, IL: University of Chicago Press.

DHSS (1983) *Social Work Decisions in Child Care – Recent Research Findings and Their Implications.* London: HMSO.

Doran, K. and Young, J. (1987) 'Child abuse: The real crisis.' *New Society,* 27 November: 10–14.

Erickson, M.H., Rossi, E. and Rossi, S. (1976) *Hypnotic Realities.* New York: Irvington.

Evans, D. and Kearney, J. (1996) *Working in Social Care: A Systemic Approach.* Aldershot: Arena.

FEU (1984) *Towards a Competency Based System.* London: FEU.

FEU (1987) *Pickup Project Report – Competency Based Vocational Training.* London: FEU.

Forrester, J.W. (1972) 'Understanding the counterintuitive behaviour of social systems.' In R.J. Beishon and G. Peters (eds) *Systems Behaviour.* London: Harper and Row.

Franklin, R. (1998) 'The SAS in cardies.' *Community Care,* 10–16 December.

Gibbs, G. (1990) *Improving Student Learning Project: Briefing Paper.* Oxford: Oxford Centre for Staff Development, Oxford Polytechnic.

Giller, H. and Morris, A. (1981) *Care and Discretion.* London: Burnett Books.

Goldner, V. (1985) 'Warning: family therapy may be hazardous to your health.' *Family Therapy Networker* 9, 6, 18–23.

Goldstein, H. (1973) *Social Work Practice.* Columbia: University of South Carolina Press.

Goolishian, H. and Winderman, L. (1988) 'Constructivism, autopoiesis and problem determined systems.' *Irish Journal of Psychology* 9, 130–43.

Griffith, J.Y., Griffith, M.E. and Slovik, L.S. (1990) 'Mind-body problems in family therapy: Contrasting first- and second-order cybernetic approaches.' *Family Process* 29, 13–28.

Haley, J. (1981) *Reflections on Therapy.* Washington, DC: Family Therapy Institute.

Haley, J. (1980a) *Leaving Home.* New York: McGraw-Hill.

Haley, J. (1976a) 'Development of a theory.' In C.E. Sluzki and D.C. Ranson (eds) *Double Bind: The foundation of the Communicational Approach to the Family.* New York: Grune and Stratton.

Haley, J. (1976b) *Problem Solving Therapy.* San Francisco, CA: Jossey Bass.

Haley, J. (1973) *Uncommon Therapy: the Psychiatric Techniques of Milton H. Erickson.* New York: Norton.

Harris, R.J. (1985) 'The transfer of learning in social work education.' In R.J. Harris (ed) *Educating Social Workers.* Leicester: Association of Teachers in Social Work Education.

Hirschi, T. (1971) *Causes of Delinquency.* California: University of California Press.

Hoffman, L. (1990) 'Constructing realities: An art of lenses.' *Family Process* 29, 1, 1–12.

Hoffman, L. (1981) *Foundations of Family Therapy – A Conceptual Framework for Systems Change.* New York: Basic Books.

Hoffman, L. and Long, L. (1969) 'A systems dilemma.' *Family Process,* September, 211–34.

Hollis, F. (1972) *Casework – A Psychosocial Therapy.* New York: Random House.

Imber-Black, E. (1988) *Families and Larger Systems.* New York: Guildford Press.

Imber-Black, E. (1986a) 'Maybe "lineal causality" needs another defense lawyer: A feminist response to Dell.' *Family Process* 25, 523–5.

Imber-Black, E. (1986b) 'The systemic consultant and human-service-provider systems.' In L.C. Wynne, S.H. McDaniel and T.T. Weber (eds) *Systems Consultation – A New Perspective for Family Therapy.* London: Guildford Press.

Imber-Coppersmith, E. (1982) 'The place of family therapy in the homeostasis of larger systems.' In Aronson and Wolberg (eds) *Group and Family Therapy: An Overview.* New York: Brunner- Mazel.

Jackson, M.C., Mansell, G.J., Flood, R.L., Blackham, R.B. and Probert, S.V.E. (eds) (1991) *Systems Thinking in Europe.* London: Plenum Press.

Johannessen, J. (1991) 'Levels of problem structuring and problem definitions.' In M.C. Jackson *et al.* (eds) *Systems Thinking in Europe.* London: Plenum Press.

Jordan, W. (1991) 'Competencies and values.' *Social Work Education* 10, 1, 5–11.

Jordan, W. (1981) 'Family therapy – an outsider's view.' *Journal of Family Therapy* 3, 269–80.

Jordan, W. and Brandon, D. (1979) *Creative Social Work.* Oxford: Basil Blackwell.

Kast, F.E. and Rosenzweig, J.E. (1972) 'The modern view: A systems approach.' In R.J. Beishon and G. Peters (eds) *Systems Behaviour.* London: Harper and Row.

Katz, D. and Kahn, R.L. (1966) *The Social Psychology of Organisations.* New York: Wiley.

Keeney, B. (1983) *Aesthetics of Change.* New York: Guilford Press.

Keeney, B.P. and Ross, J.M. (1985) *Mind in Therapy – Constructing Systemic Family Therapies.* New York: Basic Books.

Kierney, B. (1992) *The Report of the Inquiry into Child Care Policies in Fife.* Edinburgh: HMSO.

Krüll, M., Luhmann, N. and Maturana, H.R. (1989) 'Basic concepts of the theory of autopoietic systems.' *Systemic Studies* 1, 79–104.

Lettvin, J.Y., Maturana, H., McCulloch, W. and Pitts, W. (1959) 'What the frog's eye told the frog's brain.' *Proceedings of the I.R.E. 1959* 47.

Maruyama, M. (1968) 'The second cybernetics.' In W. Buckley (ed) *Modern Systems Research for the Behavioural Scientist.* Chicago, IL: Aldine.

Maturana, H.R. (1988) 'Reality: The search for objectivity or the quest for a compelling argument.' *Irish Journal of Psychology* 9, 25–82.

Matza, D. (1969) *Becoming Deviant.* Englewood Cliffs, NJ: Prentice-Hall.

McLeish, A. (1990) *An Existential Response to Competence Statements.* London: CICED.

McNamee, S. (1992) 'Reconstructing identity: The communal construction of crisis.' In S. McNamee and K.J. Gergen (eds) *Therapy as Social Construction.* London: Sage.

McNamee, S. and Gergen, K.J. (eds) *Therapy as Social Construction.* London: Sage.

Millham, S., Bullock, R. and Hosie, K. (1986) *Lost in Care.* Aldershot: Gower.

Minuchin, S. (1991) 'The seductions of constructivism.' *Networker,* September/October, 47–50.

Minuchin, S. (1974) *Families and Family Therapy.* Cambridge, MA: Harvard University Press.

Minuchin, S. and Fishman, H.C. (1981) *Family Therapy Techniques.* London: Harvard University Press.

Morgan, G. (1993) *Imaginization.* Beverly Hills, CA: Sage.

Morgan, G. (1986) *Images of Organization.* Beverly Hills, CA: Sage.

Nellis, M. (1987) 'The myth of up-tariffing in I.T.' *AJJUST* 12, 7–12.

Packman, J., Randall, J. and Jacques, N. (1986) *Who Needs Care? Social Work Decisions about Children.* Oxford: Blackwell.

Parker, J., Casburn, M. and Turnbull, D. (1981) *Receiving Juvenile Justice.* Oxford: Blackwell.

Perleman, H.H. (1957) *Social Casework: A Problem-solving Process.* Chicago, IL: University of Chicago Press.

Pincus, A. and Minahan, A. (1973) *Social Work Practice: Model and Method.* Illinois: Peacock.

Pithouse, A. (1987) *Social Work: The Social Organisation of an Invisible Trade.* Aldershot: Avebury.

Preston-Shoot, M. (1990) 'Defining the theory: A systems approach.' In D. Agass (ed) *Making Sense of Social Work.* Basingstoke: Macmillan.

Ritzer, G. (1993) *The McDonaldization of Society.* Thousand Oaks, CA: Pine Forge Press.

Rosenbleuth, A., Wiener, N. and Bigelow, J. (1968 [1943]) 'Behaviour, purpose and teleology.' In W. Buckley (ed) *Modern Systems Research for the Behavioural Scientists.* Chicago, IL: Aldine.

Ross, S. (1999a) 'What is a home help?' *Professional Social Work,* 6–7.

Ross, S. (1999b) 'Can social work ever win with the media?' Paper given at British Association for Social Workers National Conference, Southport.

Ross, S. (1987) 'Systems intervention in child care.' PhD thesis, Keele, University of Keele.

Ross, S. (1984) 'The sacred cow of IT', *Community Care,* 24–26, 16 February.

Satir, V. (1964) *Conjoint Family Therapy.* Palo Alto: Science and Behaviour Books.

Selvini-Palazzoli, M., Anolli, L., Di Blasio, P., Giossi, L., Pisano, I., Ricci, C., Sacchi, M. and Ugazio, V. (1986) *The Hidden Games of Organizations.* New York: Pantheon.

Selvini-Palazzoli M., Boscolo, L., Cecchin, G. and Prata, G. (1978) *Paradox and Counterparadox – A New Model in the Therapy of the Family in Schizophrenic Transaction.* London: Aronson.

Selvini-Palazzoli, M., Boscolo, L., Cecchin, G. and Prata G. (1980a) 'The problem of the referring person.' *Journal of Marital and Family Therapy* 6, 3–12.

Selvini-Palazzoli, M., Boscolo, L., Cecchin, G. and Prata, G. (1980b) 'Circularity – neutrality: three guidelines for the conductor of the session.' *Family Process* 19, 1, 3–12.

Sheldon, B. (1987) 'Implementing the findings of social work effectiveness research.' *British Journal of Social Work* 17, 6, 573–86.

Sinclair, R. (1987) 'Behind the numbers: An examination of child care statistics.' *Policy and Politics* 15, 2, 111–117.

Sluzki, C.E. (1988) 'Case commentary II, in constructivism applied.' *Family Therapy Networker* 12, 5, 77–9.

Spencer-Brown, G. (1973) *Laws of Form.* New York: Bantam.

Steyaert, J. (1992) 'Databases and information systems in human services: Where do we go from here?' *New Technology in the Human Services* 6, 1, 20–9.

Taylor, W.R. (1979) 'Using systems theory to organize confusion.' *Family Process* 18, 479–487.

Tebbit, N. (1997) *The Mail on Sunday,* 28 September.

Thomas, H. and Millichamp, D. (1985) 'A matter of natural justice.' *Community Care* 13 June, 25–27.

Thorpe, D.H. and Bilson, A. (1998a) 'From protection to concern: Child protection careers without apologies.' *Children and Society* 12, 373–86.

Thorpe, D.H. and Bilson, A. (1998b) 'From investigation to apology: Making sense of child protection careers.' *Children and Society* 12, 373–386.

Thorpe, D.H., Smith, D., Green, C.J. and Paley, J.H. (1980) *Out of Care: The Community Support of Juvenile Offenders.* London: George Allen and Unwin.

Tsoukas, H. (1992) 'Ways of seeing: Topographic and network representations in organization theory.' *Systems Practice* 5, 4, 441–56.

Varela, F.J. (1976) 'On observing natural systems'. *Co-Evolution Quarterly* 10, 26–31.

Walker, H. and Beaumont, B. (eds) (1985) *Working with Offenders.* Basingstoke: Macmillan.

Walrond-Skinner, S. (1981) *Developments in Family Therapy: Theories and Applications since 1948.* London: Routledge.

Walrond-Skinner, S. (1976) *Family Therapy: The Treatment of Natural Systems.* London: Routledge and Kegan Paul.

Watzlawick, P. (1978) *The Language of Change.* New York: Basic Books.

Watzlawick, P. and Weakland, J.H. (1977) *The Interactional View: Studies at the Mental Research Institute Palo Alto 1965–74.* New York: Norton.

Watzlawick, P., Weakland, J.H. and Fisch, R. (1974) *Change: Principles of Problem Formation and Resolution.* New York: Norton.

Weakland, J.H. (1981) 'A comment by John H. Weakland.' In J. Haley, *Reflections on Therapy.* Washington, DC: Family Therapy Institute.

Weber, T.T., McDaniel, S.H. and Wynne, L.C. (1986) 'Signposts for a systems consultation.' In L.C. Wynne *et al.* (eds) *Systems Consultation: A New Perspective for Family Therapy.* London: Guildford Press.

Whitehead, A.N. and Russell, B. (1910) *Principia Mathematica,* 2nd edn. Cambridge: Cambridge University Press.

Wilding, K. (1979) 'We, the willing ....' In W. Jordan and D. Brandon (eds) *Creative Social Work.* Oxford: Blackwell.

Williams, A. (1989) 'The problem of the referring person in consultancy.' *Journal of Strategic and Systemic Therapies* 8, 2, 16–21.

Wynne, L.C. (1958) 'The study of intrafamilial splits and alignments in exploratory family therapy.' In N. Ackerman (ed) *Exploring the Base for Family therapy.* New York: Family Service Association of America.

Wynne, L.C., McDaniel, S.H. and Weber, T.T. (eds) (1986) Systems Consultation – A New Perspective for Family Therapy. London: Guilford Press.

Subject Index

Name Index